AF684430

To Molly
for happy
childhood remembrances –
Ina

# Stories of a Midwest Childhood 1930s–'40s

Ina Whitlock

Also by the Author:

*Eating the Chinese Pear*
travelogue-memoir

*Of Love and Loss*
poetry

*Sketches from Paraguaná*
Venezuela, half a century ago



Published in the United States by
Spirit Journey Books, Vashon Island, Washington
iwhitlock@centurytel.net
www.InaWhitlock.com

ISBN: 978-0-9859929-0-3

Printed in the United States of America

Edited by Eagle Eye Proofreading & Editing
Book design by Novak Creative, Inc.

Front Cover Photo
"Picking Corn" iStock photo #10294798

Back Cover Photo
Dome of First United Methodist Church, Lincoln, Nebraska
Reprinted with permission of the *Lincoln Journal Star*

*"There may come to be new places in our lives that are second spiritual homes—closer to us in some ways, perhaps, than our original homes. But the home tie is the blood tie. And had it meant nothing to us, any other place thereafter would have meant less, and we could carry no compass inside ourselves to find home ever, anywhere at all. We would not even guess what we had missed."*

~ Eudora Welty

# Author’s Note

*Bree* is the me of these stories, weaving truth with imagination to give shape to days of my childhood. The stories and illustrations were conceived many years ago, and now, as I reach toward my elder-age, my hope is that such stories won’t be lost. The 1930s and ’40s were years of great social change for the nation. As a child, I saw only the changes within myself as I grew toward adulthood.

From the perspective of the 21st century, those years were a time of innocence, though, as in all times, they held hardships and corruption. The end of World War II brought great hope and rapid expansion, when it seemed that all problems could be met and overcome. We could not foresee how suddenly this era would become the technological age.

Some friends in the stories have changed identities, but all are dearly loved. As are moments we shared in the days long-lost, when we were young and growing up in Lincoln, Nebraska.

I dedicate this book to my cousins – Peggy, Loretta, and Dick – who made my childhood the longed-for great adventures of summer. And to my grandparents, whose Minnesota family farm – before the advent of electricity and a paved road – was a place of magical enchantment.

My thanks to those who have listened and commented on these stories. My special thank you to my editor, Nancy Morgan.

# Contents


The Gaillardia . . . . . . . . . . . . . . . . . . . . . . . 1

Hollyhocks . . . . . . . . . . . . . . . . . . . . . . . . . 5

Spiraea . . . . . . . . . . . . . . . . . . . . . . . . . . . 11

Four-Leaf Clover . . . . . . . . . . . . . . . . . . . . 15

Goldenrod . . . . . . . . . . . . . . . . . . . . . . . . . 19

Hay . . . . . . . . . . . . . . . . . . . . . . . . . . . . . . 25

Corn Tassels . . . . . . . . . . . . . . . . . . . . . . . 33

Poinsettia . . . . . . . . . . . . . . . . . . . . . . . . . 41

Pokeweed . . . . . . . . . . . . . . . . . . . . . . . . . 53

Lilacs . . . . . . . . . . . . . . . . . . . . . . . . . . . . 63

The Bluebell . . . . . . . . . . . . . . . . . . . . . . . 69

Seeds of the Apple . . . . . . . . . . . . . . . . . . 77

Poppies . . . . . . . . . . . . . . . . . . . . . . . . . . . 83

The White Rose . . . . . . . . . . . . . . . . . . . . . 87

Pine Clearing . . . . . . . . . . . . . . . . . . . . . . . 93

Weeping Willow . . . . . . . . . . . . . . . . . . . . 103

The Tomato . . . . . . . . . . . . . . . . . . . . . . . 113


All illustrations are by the author.

# The Gaillardia

Grimy fingers closed over the neck of the gaillardia. A small hand yanked. The flower resisted, then broke at the slender stem. For a moment, dozens of gaillardias, flags of red and yellow, quivered in the still, hot air, then fell back, leaves drooping. But bees, shaken from hiding places, rose noisily, searching here, there, finding honey at the gaillardias' dark button centers. A bee settled on the flower in her hand, sucking honey, like she sucked a milkshake through a straw. But honey at the center of the gaillardia was warm and icky. Bree fingered each yellow-tipped red petal of the flower, counting, "one, two, three, four."

Today she was four years old! Mother had sent her into the yard to play while she made a birthday cake. Leaning over the fence by the alley, trying to be nice, she told the garbage-collector man that today was her birthday.

"Well, well, sweetheart, how old are you?"

"Four!" He reached into the pocket of his overalls and handed her four pennies. "Happy Birthday!" Then he jumped on the back of the garbage truck and it rattled on down the alley. The four pennies clinked softly in her fist, but Mother said, "You should NOT have taken money from that man!"

Something cut inside her, a knife, like the pointed petal of a gaillardia. "That man is poor and needs the pennies."

And she would give them back—if she could find them. Maybe they were hidden someplace dark, but she couldn't think where. She stood by the gaillardias, closing her eyes against the sun. Inside herself she felt a drum beating, her heart ticking, like the big clock over the kitchen table—ticking, Mother said, even when she wasn't there to hear. Mother was in the kitchen now, making the cake that Bree wasn't supposed to "bother." Her birthday cake! She had waited *so* long. How many times, when she went to the screen door to ask, had Mother said, "Wait a minute, just one minute more!"

Bree pulled four petals from the gaillardia in her hand. It became a lady's red skirt with yellow rickrack at the hem. A pretty skirt for the red shoes that Miss Spivey next door sometimes let her put on. But how many birthdays until she *really* could wear high heels?

"Just a minute," said Miss Spivey, and brought the shoes to her.

A bee stopped buzzing around her to walk on the flower button in Bree's hand. She laughed. The bee looked like Mother's lady friend in her furry coat, round and fuzzy, head nodding up and down, yes, yes, just like the lady. But then the bee flew off faster than a dart going to a bull's-eye. But she didn't know where the bee went. It got lost in sunlight.

And where could she go? Never farther than the gate with a rusty latch that she couldn't open. But Indians could go anywhere. Mother said that they had lived here in her own yard, but a long time ago, before the fence and the gate.

Bree pulled a feather from an Indian headdress, then the gaillardia was a crown belonging to a princess like Miss Spivey, with her red shoes, powder boxes, and sweet smells. Miss Spivey once came toward her, tipping one of the bottles to her finger to put some of the sweet smell on Bree, but she shook her head no.

"But I want to, dear," Miss Spivey said. Maybe, then, the man *wanted* to give her four pennies. So wasn't it alright to take them? Bree pulled the remaining petals from the gaillardia, letting them fall through her fingers like pennies. She dropped the naked gaillardia and ran off into the enlarging green spaces of the garden.

# Hollyhocks

She knew all the backyards on her alley. Picking hollyhocks there, by the garage, she piled pink, white, and violet petticoats on top of each other to make dressed-up dolls. When she found milkweed, she broke a stem and, with the sticky white juice, scratched a B on her arm, then sprinkled it with Nebraska dirt to mark who she was. But today her destination – running fast because the bricks under her feet were hot – was the Methodist church, the fortress at the end of the alley.

She bounded up the wide, stone stairway to giant pillars that guarded entry to the church. But first, she grabbed a handrail at the middle of the stairs and, hooking her knees over the railing, shinnied down. Wearing her 'Sunday dress,' she had to try when her mother wasn't looking or she would say, "Don't show your panties, Bree," or "Watch out, you're going to crack your head on the steps!"

Today, she pushed hard against one of the big doors barring entrance to the church, until she could wedge a shoulder, then turning, push with her fanny until she could thrust herself into the dark inside. Bree often struggled against the mysteries of the Methodist church. First, a flash of sunlight under her eyelids, then she was able to see the doorways into the 'sank-chew-airy'.

More times than people knew, she explored shadowy stairways and cool caves to an underground kitchen where tiny windows near the ceiling gave the only light. She dodged monsters behind scattered chairs on her way through the dark, trying to find a light switch. Sometimes, where the Sunday school rooms were, she found the piano that kept getting moved. She tapped one note softly as a mouse and, if she heard no person coming, she would strike more keys, louder, then listen for footsteps.

Once, he found her hiding under a table. The minister's voice cut through the shadowy space between them. "Bree, if you don't stop trespassing, I will have to call your mother on the telephone. Do you understand?"

Bree wasn't sure what 'trespassing' was, but on Sundays the minister always said, "Welcome to God's House." And wasn't she there now, looking for Him?

She thrilled to sneak into the sank-chew-airy where colored pieces of glass made pictures of Jesus and sheep in the windows, and the front of the church was covered with pipes of a great organ. Bree scuffed her bare feet on the carpet to the altar where last Sunday's flowers drooped. The big, gold cross was on the altar. She put her fingerprints on it, and then sat down in a pew. She hated that word – pew – for the long benches with songbooks on them. But she sat down and stretched her neck, looking straight up to the dome (that's what Mother called it) at the top of the church, and there was Abraham Lincoln staring down at her, just like God. She knew that God lived in Lincoln, Nebraska, too, like she did. But Abraham Lincoln was dead and in heaven.

On Sundays, choir singing floated down to her from the church loft. She climbed the narrow stairway. There was no escape. She heard slow footsteps coming up the stairs and Miss Grace, breathing heavily. "Somebody up there, up in the choir loft?"

Silence. "Bree, is that you?"

She knew that Miss Grace was too big to bend over and look under the choir seats, so she kept silent, except for her thumping heart.

"Who's there?" A pause—then Miss Grace's heavy footsteps clump, clump, clumped down the stairs.

Other places in the Methodist church had escape ways leading into halls where she could run, feet paddling on cold floors, arms rowing fast to a safe shore beyond the stairs. She could flee – stifling a giggle – even when she was scared.

She pushed hard with her fanny against the big oak door. It gave way and she was out, never daring to look back in case Miss Grace was at the office window looking down at her.

~

A certain Sunday seemed like all the rest, the edge of a wooden pew cutting into her legs. Sitting forward, she had put her elbows on the back of the pew in front of her. Her nose caught in the veiling of a lady's hat. The lady turned a bird eye to Bree. She tried sitting cross-legged on the hard bench, pulling her skirt down around her knees. Mother took a pad and pencil from her purse, then Bree drew pictures of holy ghosts. She knew about them from Halloween. The pencil slipped, marking the songbook, but Mother didn't see.

Bree looked up to the great dome. Abraham Lincoln was looking down on her. Mother said that he was the President who freed the slaves. She didn't know what 'slaves' were, but free meant that nobody could tell you what to do or where you couldn't go. The minister was saying, "Now, let us all bow our heads in prayer. Our Father..."

How could God be everybody's father? *Her* father was sitting right by her mother with his eyes closed.

"And forgive us our trespasses," said the minister. To forgive meant not to be mad at anybody, but trespasses?

She felt her forehead wrinkle when she was trying to figure things out. Then Mother would say, "Don't scowl, Bree!"

The minister continued, "...as we forgive those who trespass against us."

"Bree, don't trespass in the church anymore!" That's what Mother had told her. Had the minister called Mother on the telephone like he said he would? Was he standing up there right now talking about *her?* Bree opened one eye and looked around, but everyone's head was bowed and no one was looking at her as if the minister *meant* her.

Sometimes she thought that Sunday church would never end, except for the songs. Bree loved being in church when the organ played and she could sing. The organist struggled onto the bench, raised her arms, and the music began. The big, low notes trembled, rumbling inside her, and then she was able to unbend her knees, stand up, and open the songbook. She knew the tunes and some of the words by heart. Sounds of the organ rolled through her in thunderous waves. She took a deep breath and sang, "God will take ca-er ov uuu..."

The music went faster, softer. "...in ev-ry way, through ev-ry day..." She loved the fluttering part where the little blackbird notes sat on the telephone lines in the songbook. "Ee willll..." The notes were rising higher. "...take ca-er of youuuu."

She felt free like the angels and maybe the slaves, too, free to do anything she wanted. She sang louder, her voice going right up to Abraham Lincoln.

"Bree, stop that!" whispered Mother. The lady with the bird eye turned to look at her and others, too, some smiling, not singing at all.

She wanted to rub the hurt away, but it came stinging

into her eyes. Something caught in her throat. Bree couldn't sing anymore, but hard as she tried, she couldn't keep the music out. It was inside her.

# Spiraea

There it was. The piano lady playing for the hop, hop, leap. Or was it hop, hop, skip? Miss Virginie said, "Alright girls, line up! Here we go!"

Bree scurried across the dance floor in her ballet slippers. She curled her toes to keep the slippers on because they were loose and the tie had a knot.

"One, two, three, four, step, step, skip, step," said Miss Virginie. She made the girls line up and follow each other, giving Bree a chance to watch the others and try to get the steps right. Her best friend, Betty, was always second in line because Betty was good at skipping and just the right size.

"Right foot, Bree, right! Left, skip—right, skip, left, skip. Circle around the room. Follow Jane and Betty, girls! That's nice. Keep in line, single file!"

Then Jane and Betty cut diagonally across the room. Bree was heading straight for the piano-playing lady and she had trouble. She was hopping up when the girl in front of her was down. She ran a pace to catch up.

"Bree, what's the matter? Watch! Watch!"

The other girls had started toward her from the opposite corner. "Girls!" Miss Virginie clapped her hands. "Quiet!"

The girls stopped. Miss Virginie stood with her ballet-shoed feet apart, her hands on her hips. "Now, we will all skip—just plain skip."

Bree looked at the long lacy curtains covering the front windows, keeping summer out.

"Bree? Can you do that? Just skip?" Sometimes she could, sometimes she couldn't, and it seemed the harder she tried, the worse she skipped. Betty's yellow curls were in front of her with her arms out so, like Miss Virginie's. Bree skipped and felt her leg almost give way—something about skipping. Miss Virginie was at her again, saying, "Bree, just relax. Have a good time!"

Bree couldn't. After the *Humoresque,* she felt the tears come when Miss Virginie said, "Bree, why don't you go outside in the driveway and practice skipping until I call you back. Now, hurry along!"

Bree got out of there as fast as she could. She pushed open the screen door, then ran down the cement steps and hid under a spiraea bush, like the one she had at home. Tears fell from her eyes. She didn't have a shirt with sleeves to stop them, so she rubbed her wrists against her eyes. If she could just skip, she wouldn't be wishing for a handkerchief because her nose was running.

When Mother first said, "You're going to dancing class," Bree shook her head NO.

"But dancing will help you to be graceful, and not trip over things. Besides, Betty is going." Only because Betty was her best friend, Bree said she would go—but she didn't like dancing any better.

She crawled further under the spiraea bush and sat there with her arms around her legs. She listened to the familiar music plunked by the piano lady in the dance room. The fast beats – six, ONE, two, three, four, five, six – of the Mexican Hat Dance they would do for the recital. Dancing around her hat, she had slipped accidentally and stepped on it, but Miss Virginie had picked the hat up and punched it out again. Then Miss Virginie gave her a different part. Now, she play-fought with a boy from the other class and, at the end, he dragged her off the stage by one leg.

Through lacy windows of the spiraea, Bree heard the waltz. She could dance to the waltz because she knew, even better than Betty, the ONE, two, three beat of the music. But she wasn't inside today (like last time) to surprise Miss Virginie and hear her say, "That's right, Bree!"

She reached through the branches for some of the tiny flowers that made little bouquets for an imaginary dollhouse. There would be a tiny piano, her fingers sprinkling the keys with music.

~

Voices were calling: "Bree! Bree! Where are you?"

How did she get there, under the spiraea? Then Bree remembered her shame.

"Shame on you!" they'd say. And she hadn't practiced skipping once! Should she stay there and not get scolded, or 'face the music' as Mother had said when Bree hid two quarters under her bed instead of putting them back in Mother's purse? She *was* bad, sometimes. And worst of all, bad at skipping.

When footsteps and those calling her had moved down the driveway, Bree pushed back the spiraea branches and skipped as hard as she could until somebody said, "There you are!"

Betty said, "Your mommy's here!"

Bree told herself that she would practice all week skipping one foot and then the other and then Miss Virginie wouldn't notice her at all.

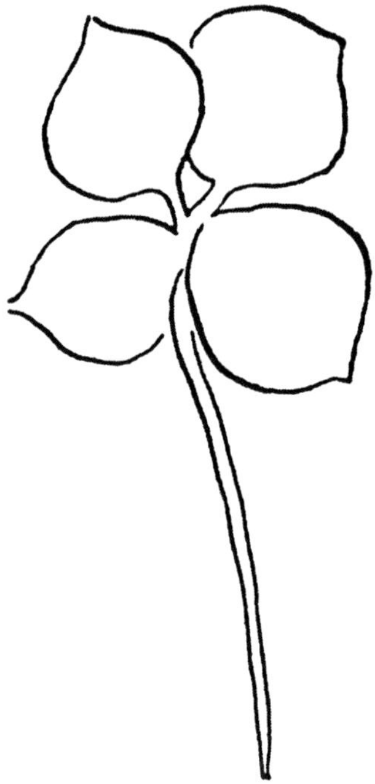

# Four-Leaf Clover

Her fingers searched the grass for a lucky four-leaf clover. Untangling the clover, she found the one stem with four leaves. She was lucky today! Bree unfastened the buckle of her new school shoe and slipped the clover under her heel, then struggled to get her heel back into the shoe. She struggled even more to pull the strap through far enough to catch the buckle.

Mother came out of the house. "Bree, for heaven's sake, what are you doing? Taking off your shoe?"

"No. Putting it on!"

"But I thought you were ready to go!"

Bree was the one who was ready to go, the one who had waited so long in the yard for Mother to come out.

"Let's get going," said Mother. Bree pushed open the rusty latch of the gate. "Walking to your first day of school. What do you think of that, Bree?"

"I don't know," she said, stopping to pull up her new, white knee socks. But she couldn't remember not wanting to go to school. She had waited and waited.

She remembered waiting all afternoon on the porch steps to see Shirley Temple dance and sing in a movie. No calls from Mother to "Come away from there" or "Bree, it's hours before we go"—nothing could keep Bree from waiting.

Mother had tried to curl Bree's hair like Shirley Temple's, with a hot curling iron, but that hadn't worked, so Bree got her hair cut 'Dutch boy' style. After that, whenever Bree dressed special, like today, Mother fastened a big plaid bow in her hair. For Christmas, she got a Shirley Temple doll with curls all over her head. But the doll would stay home today, when Bree went to school.

Mother stopped at the corner for a car to pass. “Bree, you will have to look both ways before you cross the street. Do you understand? You’re a big girl, now. I can’t be with you all the time to tell you *No*.”

Bree pulled her hand from Mother’s and slipped it into the pocket of her new dress. She would have to wear dresses to school and that meant that her panties would show if she played on the hand bars. And she wouldn’t be home mornings, either, to ride her tricycle. She wouldn’t be there when the street-cleaning machine came by, the big brushes sweeping the dirt and smaller, wet brushes gobbling up the dust and leaves.

Imagining her tricycle as a street cleaner, she had punched holes in paper cups and tied them to her tricycle. She filled the cups with water from the garden hose and cleaned the sidewalk in front of her house. The street-cleaner man waved to her as he passed on his big monster machine.

“Can you walk home all by yourself?” asked Mother.

“Ummhumm.” Bree stretched as tall as she could, taking hold of Mother’s hand as they climbed the cement steps of the school. When the door to the kindergarten room opened, she was pulling up her socks.

“Bree, this is your teacher.”

Bree stood up and looked at the tall lady. “I’m Miss Hatch. Your name is...?”

“Bree.”

“Bree?” The lady looked hard at her.

"Uh huh!"

"Bree," said Mother, "you must answer, 'Yes, Miss Hatch.' Remember that!"

"Yes, Miss Hatch," she said, looking past her into the room where children were climbing boxes, sweeping, hammering, fitting puzzles, playing store. She ran across the floor to a table piled with books.

"Bree!" called Mother. "You mustn't run in class!"

"Uh uh—no, Mother."

"Be a good girl, now." Mother turned to leave, but Bree followed her and pulled on her sleeve until Mother bent down. Bree whispered, "But does Shirley Temple have to go to school?"

"Of course she does!" said Mother. "What a silly question!"

It wasn't until Miss Hatch gave everyone cymbals and bells to march around the school room that Bree had to pull up her socks again, and that is when she remembered the lucky four-leaf clover in her shoe.

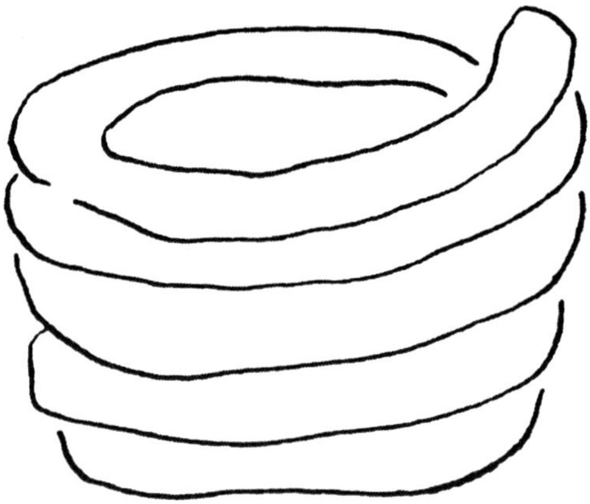

# Goldenrod

"The old Muddy Blue hasn't overflowed this year," said Father, looking down at the lazy, brown ribbon of river. He stood on the riverbank, where sun made all the feathery goldenrod around him even more golden. Everybody else was lazing on blankets in the heat of the day.

Bree stood poking a stick into clay just below the surface of the water. She was looking for tadpoles to put in a paper cup she'd saved from the picnic lunch.

Poking brought up no tadpoles, but the grey mud she found was fine for making Indian pots. Bree dug her hands into the muck, bringing up squishy globs. Muddy water splat through her fingers as she clenched her fists. The mud soon dried enough to make 'snakes' that she could coil into pots.

She sat by the Muddy Blue making pots just as the Indians did long ago. But then, picnickers' cars weren't parked just off the country road. Horses, palomino horses, were standing over yonder. Her tribe was up there, asleep on blankets above the riverbank. She was the scout, waiting for an enemy or maybe a friendly Indian to pass. She knew that beyond the bend in the river, a bridge of jumping stones would let her cross to the other side when the water was low, like now.

Bree set her Indian pots in a row on the riverbank and climbed around the bend of the pokey Blue – carefully – as the bank was steep. The river didn't seem to want to go anywhere, but her father said that it flowed into the Platte River, and that flowed into the Missouri, and from there, into the Mighty Mississippi.

Father said that small streams are "like capillaries, the Platte and the Missouri are the veins, and the Mighty Mississippi is the artery of this great country."

Bree looked for the veins in her arms, but they were covered with mud. She touched the spot on her wrist where she could feel her blood flow. She was flowing into the future, but she wouldn't know, because it would seem just like today.

She grabbed at grasses and goldenrod to keep from slipping into the river. Rounding the next bend, there might be someone waiting for her, to speak Indian with her. She tried a few phrases for sound.

"Oma tiki poo—how!" she said, raising her hand straight up from the elbow. She tried again, louder this time. "Tiki tipoo wahoo—how!" Up jerked her arm, but no one was on the opposite bank to greet her (as she half expected), though grasses waved like feathers of an Indian headdress. Indians hid there, somewhere, waiting for her to pass—to trespass.

"Wahoo, Shawnee, Cheyenne, Ogallala, Omaha," she sang. The bridge of stones invited her to cross to the other side. To be an Indian brave, she'd have to take off her shirt, so she tossed it on the bank. She had her berry basket paper cup fastened in the elastic of her shorts.

Arms outspread to balance, she crossed on the stones. A tribe on the bank was looking on to see if she would find berries, but she only found cockleburs that pricked and stuck to the pants and socks of 'palefaces.' She pulled a painful sticker from her bare big toe. But Indians could glide through anything and not get caught or make a sound. But if they called to her, she would answer, "Billa Willa," a good girl-boy name.

Bree knew that Indians look to the sky for signs. The

stars at night are a reading book. In sun time, clouds tell the stories. "But you must never look directly into the sun," said Father. She had tried it, though, and got fire in her eyes.

She looked now at the little white lambs in the sky that were getting softer and muddier, even some black sheep coming over the field of clouds – signs the Indians knew – and to her it looked like a storm, dark to the north with the wind blowing up. Grass rippled in front of her and almost made her dizzy. She put a finger in her mouth then held it to the wind.

Patting her palm back and forth on her mouth, she shouted, "Ow-wow-wow-wow!"

From far away the rumble of drums – Indian drums – answered her. She galloped through the grass as the wind picked up. At the riverbank, she slid off her horse Indian-style, feet together, then let her palomino roam free.

She'd better get out of there. It was starting to rain. Bree scrambled down the bank. The river was muddier than before, with big storm clouds overhead, and the wind making ripples on the water. She heard thunder, like a big drum. And lightning flashes, crashing like cymbals.

Bree hopped along, crossing over the stones to the other side as fast as she could. Big splotches of rain fell, but the wind and thunder let up for a moment and Bree thought the weather was going to clear. She climbed around the bend of the river, grabbing for goldenrod at the top of the bank, pulling down clods as the roots let go. Her foot slipped and she was in the water, but only to her knees.

Suddenly, rain came down as she ran along the bank, rain flowers and Indian beads falling all over her. She put her hand to her mouth. "Ow-wow-wow-wow!"

"Youu-hoo! Bree is that you?"

That was the tribe in the distance. “Billa Willa,” she answered.

She tried to scramble up the bank, but it was slippery with rain. The trickles that come before capillaries were falling into the Muddy Blue and she wasn’t able to get up. Bree dug her toes in and then her knees. If the river rose, she would have to get up fast. Grabbing at roots and goldenrod at the top of the bank, she pulled herself up over the edge.

Through strings of wet hair, she saw Mother standing over her, wrapped in a blanket.

“For heaven’s sake, where have you been? You look like an Indian! You worried us in this storm. Your father went out to look for you and found your shirt on the riverbank. How can you be so careless?”

Bree sat on a blanket in the backseat of the car as Father drove through the rain on a county road, taking her farther and farther from the old Muddy Blue. She sang to herself, “Billa Willa, Billa Willa... Billa... Will...”

# Hay

Bree was where she most wanted to be, ever. She dreamed of it all winter long. She wanted to be on Grandma's farm in the summer, playing with her cousins. And here she was, with her cousin Retta, up in the hayloft in the barn, trying to figure out what to play next. They had put the decision to each other – what to vote for – corncob dolls, sing what is the tune, Sears & Roebuck paper dolls, or drop the cat out of the loft. (They had tried that once, and the cat had shaken its head and walked away, to her great relief.)

Bree felt herself sink into a pile of hay in the hayloft. "I want to play cowboys," she said to Retta. "Roy Rogers!"

Of all her cowboy heroes, Bree liked him best: that always cheerful, friendly smile and Roy Rogers always knowing what to do, except, maybe, for kissing girls. He looks out from the movie screen with pale eyes and says in the nicest way, "Howdy, pahdnah" and "Ah think it's time ah saunter down to the OK Corral. Smiley, you comin?"

"I'm Roy Rogers!" said Bree, sliding off the hay.

"But I ain't gonna be Smiley, no way!" said Retta. "You can't have all them best parts."

"That – ain't – no best part," said Bree, feeling the *ain't* stick on her tongue. "It's just I'm always Roy Rogers. Can't be anybody else!"

"No? Why not?"

Bree felt something grab at her chest, like a bottle blown around a ship; a little panic of emotion got caught in her throat and couldn't get out. She *had* to be Roy Rogers.

"…'sides, I'm the only one of us sings good like him."

"He don't hafta sing!"

"But he *does* sing, in every movie!"

"You seen 'em all?"

"Well, no, maybe…"

"Then how come you say so? Don't hafta be."

"Why not?"

"I dunno—I just dunno who ta be," said Retta, sitting cross-legged in clumps of straw, her elbows on her knees, hands cupping her chin.

"Be the Lone Ranger, then. He's got Tonto, like I got Smiley. We gotta be equal, don't we?"

"But the Lone Ranger ain't equal!"

Bree sat back down on the hay. This was going to take longer than she thought. "Why ain't he equal?"

"Ya only hear 'im on the radio, ya don't get ta see 'im in the movies."

"But Retta, you being the Lone Ranger, get to say loud, so everybody can hear, 'Hi Ho Silver! The Lone Ranger rides again!' You get a silver horse with the speed of lightning, too."

"Well," said Retta, brushing strands of red hair from her freckled forehead, "I don't wanna."

Bree pulled a straw from the haystack and chewed on it like she'd seen the other fellows do in the cowboy movies.

"Well, what's Roy Rogers' horse like, then?" Retta asked.

"It's only a kinda light brown color with a yellow mane and tail."

"I like that horse better."

"But Retta, if you play the Lone Ranger, you get a mask! We both get cowboy hats and boots, but you're the only one gets a mask, a bandana over your face. I guess I don't, 'cause I gotta sing once in a while... Come on, Retta, be him!"

"Naw, I don't wanna."

"Alright then, you be Hopalong Cassidy! He's even got two names you can say all together—William Boyd Hopalong Cassidy."

"But I don't know him."

"He's the best cowboy there is!"

"Does he wear them silver buckles and stuff?"

"He's even got silver spurs – you know what I mean – kicks his horse and makes him go faster."

"What's his name?"

"William Boyd Hopalong Cassidy."

"No! I mean his horse."

"Well, I don't know. It's a white horse, so it must be Snowball, you know, so fast it goes like a cannonball." Bree saw that Retta didn't like that. "Ping-pong! That's a good name. Real fast and pure white."

"But I don't wanna be Hopalong!"

"Yes you do! He wears this black mask with circles around his eyes and he wears a black cowboy outfit and a black cowboy hat. Not many cowboys have them, you know. In fact, I can't think of one other cowboy who wears a black hat."

"I don't care!"

"He even shoots better than Roy Rogers."

"...'cause he don't hafta sing them dumb songs!"

"They're not dumb! It's just Roy Rogers sings instead of shoots. Besides, Hopalong has two guns, and he gets all the bad guys."

"Can't he have some *good* guys working for him too?"

"Okay, you take a bunch of good guys, as many as you want, and I'll take Smiley and we can get our horses and head for the OK Corral, okay?"

"But what ranch belongs to me?"

"It's a big one. Guess they got about a million steers on the property."

"Bigger 'an Grandma's?"

"Yes, Dumbo – I mean Hopalong – they got about a million acres."

"Wow! I'll keep my horse in that empty cow stall," said Retta.

"Me too!"

"No ya don't. There must be lotsa other places in these million acres."

"Okay," sighed Bree, "I'll keep mine in the shed—the OK Corral shed."

"Ain't there some old saddles in there?"

"Maybe, let's go!" Roy Rogers followed Hopalong Cassidy down the ladder from the hayloft. Cows not out to pasture mooed heavily as the girls climbed down.

"Reckon them bandits'll show up soon."

"Right-o, pahdnah."

Finally, Retta was going to be Hopalong. "I gotta get my

two-guns," she said, heading at a gallop for the pine forest at the edge of the farmyard.

The old homestead was built, Grandma said, by Bree's great grandfather, the first pioneer settler in Linwood County, Minnesota. It was a two-storied clapboard house with wide screened porches, front and back. Sandy paths wandered from the house to the barn, the corncrib, and the shed. Bree kicked around in the shed where old pieces of farm machinery were stored: the grinding stone, rusty buckets of rusty nails, and pegs with halters and reins for the horse team, but there was no old saddle in the shed.

Bree liked best being free like now – to be whoever she wanted – and mostly she wanted to be like—she wanted to *be* Roy Rogers. She didn't want to be Dale Evans, at all, in her fringy cowgirl skirt, waiting for the men to come home – her man – Roy, to dish him up some soup or something or maybe get a barbeque ready and checkered tablecloths. Like when somebody picks a fight and knocks over the table and the beer, two mean guys fighting over Dale Evans and 'who gets her'—gets her to fix supper, they mean. Then Roy comes riding in from the range not knowing anything's wrong, and he pulls out his guitar and starts singing a song. Then the fight's over and everybody joins in the singing around the barbeque, Roy Rogers' horse smiling over Roy's shoulder and Smiley at his side, and Roy singing:

(She had to make up the words.)

"I'm just a lonely cowboy

a ridin' on the range

the years go by I'm ridin'

ain't nothin' ever change,

...'til I meet my true love

under starry skies above

I'm just a lonely cowboy

and tonight I'll hit the hay.

Yippy yi yo, yippy yi yea

Yippy yo ki yo, yippy yi yo ki yea."

The only time Bree might want to be Dale Evans is when Smiley says, "Come on, Roy," and brings him up to her and says, "Go on, Roy," and Roy Rogers kisses Dale Evans on the cheek as the movie fades and the singing comes up big, "Yippy yi yo ki yea..."

"Hey, Bree!"

"Yeh?"

"I don't wanna play no more. Can't find no sticks—no two-guns, I mean."

"Well, I just found this rifle." Bree picked up an old hammer handle from dead leaves and pine needles under her feet.

Retta said, "Can't play unless Hopalong's got two guns, besides, I'm hungry anyway."

"Yeah, me too. Let's go down to the chuck wagon. Okay?"

"I'm Hopalong, you're Roy. Okay?"

"Okay."

From the chuck wagon down at the OK Corral, the smell of freshly baked bread filled Bree with a special way of being happy. Grandma called, "Wipe the sand off your feet, girls, and shut the screen door. Don't let them flies in!"

# Corn Tassels

Sand pushed up between her toes as she walked a long row in the cornfield. Cornstalks above her rustled papery, dry husks cut against her bare shoulders. Harvesting would come soon. Most of the corn tassels had dried curly black, but prettier ones were still purple or brown, like the 'henna ladies' at the beauty parlor where she had to look through magazines all afternoon while Mother's hair was washed, colored, curled, and dried. The corncob tassels looked very much like ladies' hair, especially when the corn was young, almost as yellow-green as Betty's hair after camp last summer. The swimming pool had turned her blond curls green, and then she had to get her hair washed every day. Betty was not as lucky as Bree, not having a grandma's farm to come to in the summer.

Bree lay down in the cornfield, into the feel of warm sand—her body sinking as low as she could into the earth, her cheek in the soft Minnesota sandy soil. She was playing hide-and-seek with her cousins. She listened. No sound but the occasional lazy rustle of a cornstalk. Then she heard Retta and Dickie making smashing noises not far away.

"Ouch!"

"Ah, whydcha havta do that!" Retta cried. "Ain't fair!"

"Is too!"

"No tain't. Get offa me then, Dumbo!"

"Dumbo? Where'd ya get that? Caught ya din' I?"

"But ain't fair ta tackle me. We ain't playing football!"

"But I caught ya. You're *It*!"

"No I ain't! Ain't gonna play if you don't play fair!"

Bree got up, disgusted. If they couldn't make a good game, she didn't want to play, either. Sure enough, two rows over, her cousin Dickie was sprawled over his sister, Retta, tangled in cornstalks.

"Get up, Dickie! I ain't gonna lay here forever, you know. Gee! What is Uncle gonna say about the busted corn?" Retta managed to get onto her knees, brushing sand from her face. "Gee whiz!"

Bree looked at the mangled corn. Two corncobs projected at angles where the stalk had broken. Bree pulled back the husks, the blankets covering the corn. The kernels were hard. In the early summer, she ate raw new kernels. They had a sweet, floury taste, but now the corncobs made good dolls. She broke one free from the stalk. "Hey Retta, let's play corncob dolls."

"Okay, but ya know how Uncle gets mad if we go around messing things up—like Dickie, wrecking the cornfield."

"It ain't wrecked."

"Well, you sure wrecked our game! Ain't gonna play with you no more. Gonna play corncob dolls."

"Come on, can't I play witcha?"

"You'd only wreck it up."

Sometimes Dickie did cause trouble, just being a boy. Cousin Peg was somebody else. She was the oldest of the three cousins and wandered away when she didn't want to play anymore. Retta would ask Peg to play with them, to get things for them like empty bottles or flour sacks for playing house. Peg could beg cookies off Grandma better than Bree or Retta. Grandma always said to the two of them, "Well, girls, what are you up to this time?"

After looking at each other, one would ask for something to eat, or some scraps of material, whatever Bree and Retta had in mind to do at that moment. Often Grandma was at the big black stove, feeding it pieces of wood, her round body tied in an apron, her face pink from the heat. Sometimes she was at the pump in the milk room off the kitchen and she'd say, "Come here, Bree, and pump this water for me."

Grandma was proud for having an indoor pump. Bree would take the pump handle and pull it down and push it up again, stretching all the muscles in her arms, until she could jump up with the handle and pull it down hard. When the pump gained momentum and the handle came down easily, from deep in the ground – in a big gush – out rushed sparkling cold water.

Bree placed a bucket under the spout. The basin was speckled grey all over where Uncle in his overalls came in from milking the cows and washed up, lathering his sunburnt face and arms in soap and rinsing all at once, splashing water everywhere, drying himself on an old grey towel, and then he would sit down to a breakfast of six eggs and bacon and six slices of Grandma's bread and blackberry jam, after eating a big bowl of oatmeal. Bree tried, but she couldn't eat half as much as Uncle, even when she was very hungry, though everything tasted twice as good at Grandma's as anywhere else.

Bree carried the bucket to the kitchen. "Hey, Grandma, here's the water!"

Grandma fed the water into the hot water reservoir of the big, black stove. Bree rarely found her anywhere else but cooking, except once, when Bree went all the way out to the outhouse and flung open the door, to find Grandma sitting there looking at the old Sears & Roebuck catalogue.

Sometimes after lunch, she might find Grandma sitting

in a straight chair on the front screened porch cleaning 'ick' off eggs before putting them in cartons for market. Sometimes Bree had to sit there with a wet rag and help.

Grandma always listened for any car that might pass on the road. "Yes, sir," she'd say, "that sounds like the Richardsons coming," and seconds later the old Richardson Chevrolet would come into sight, wheels churning up sand. "Sure enough, musta been up ta their daughter's; she's just got a new baby," or "Old Man Johnson died, so they prob'ly went to visit the family."

All activity stopped and everyone waved when a car went by or, as likely, stopped in to "pass the time" as Grandma said. Exciting as it was when cookies or cake were served on the porch, the most fun for Bree was making up something to do with Retta, or the whole gang playing games. But games usually got messed up – like hide-and-seek in the cornfield – and never came out like she wanted, except when they played 'Major Bowes Amateur Hour' (the real shows were on the radio). Then the cousins performed for the adults after dinner: silly skits that always broke up in giggles, or somebody saying the parts of a poem they could remember, or Bree singing a song. She was pretty good with cowboy songs, but always impatient waiting for her turn on stage.

Today, Grandma was at the stove, as usual, cooking things for dinner, keeping the fire going even in the summer, stew simmering on top, biscuits and blueberry muffins baking, and bread rising, to turn golden brown inside the oven.

"Grandma," said Retta, "can we look in your closet?"

"Been meaning to get in there and clean it out – but somehow – whatever do you want to look in there for, girls?"

"Me and Bree jus' wanna find stuff ta make dolls. You know—that bag of sewing scraps and jars of buttons. Can we look through 'em?"

"Don't matter to me, girls. Do what you want."

That was what Bree loved most about Grandma's. They were free to do mostly what they wanted. She and Retta had spent a whole rainy morning from breakfast until lunch in the closet. The shelves were filled with boxes and jars of all kinds. The girls had pulled out old Sears and Roebuck catalogues to sit on and had looked through faded photographs of ladies in puffy sleeves, with tiny waists and big hats with feathers, and men in stiff, round collars. None of the people seemed to be smiling and Bree couldn't understand why. It would be fun to dress up like that. Maybe they were sad because most of them were dead now. That wasn't really right, but it seemed an explanation. They were part of a family and she was part of that family. But she couldn't pick out which of them were related to her any more than she could have picked out into which family she was born.

Retta found the bag of sewing scraps. They chose material for the corncob dolls, cutting a slot for the neck of the dresses. They collected ribbons, buttons, and pins. "Got 'um!" said Retta.

"Wait a minute," said Bree. "We've got to get some toothpicks."

"Yeah, almost forgot their arms," said Retta.

They looked in the pantry. It was filled to the top with good things—blue Mason jars of fruits and vegetables that Grandma fixed all by herself, pickle jars, barrels of flour, pitchers of souring milk, a butter churn and bread tins, and enough cooking pans to feed the dozen extra neighbors who come when it is time to harvest the corn. Sometimes Bree lay on the cot on the porch by the pantry window with all the good smells of the kitchen and pantry coming to her through the open window, the smells sweet and salty and doughy all at once. The cats climbed up on the cot with her, waving their tails, settling down in round balls beside her. She would lullaby them, "My pretty babies, go to sleep." But sometimes the cats weren't so pretty, when they were loose in the pantry with a mouse.

Finding toothpicks there was like finding needles in a haystack. She looked everywhere. "Look on the pantry shelf by the door, halfway up," called Grandma.

Bree and Retta grabbed a dozen toothpicks to make arms for the corncob dolls and extras to chew, just as they'd seen Uncle do when he perched back on the chair legs, rubbed his stomach and said, "Mighty good meal, Ma!"

Back in the cornfield, Bree and Retta searched through the rows. "They ought to be about here."

"But they ain't."

"Let's look once more." Bree went one direction, Retta another, looking for the knocked-over cornstalks. But the rows looked the same: straight, leaves full, stalks taller than Bree.

"Hey, Retta, find them?"

"Naw," yelled Retta. They called to each other up and down the rows, each following the other's voice until they met somewhere in the middle of the cornfield.

"Forget it. Let's just pick the best dolls. The prettiest hair."

"Let's fix them up in the corncrib, okay?"

"Okay."

The dolls in their arms, Retta led Bree out of the corn.

The corncrib was empty except for the smell of last year's

corn and a few dried kernels in cracks of the floor. Bree hoped they would not be bothered by Dickie or Peg saying how dumb corncob dolls were, because she thought her dolls were quite beautiful. She tied their hair with ribbons, pushed toothpicks into the cobs for arms, dressed them in flowery material, and tied their waists with ribbon.

The girls played in the corncrib the rest of the afternoon, making up stories to play with brunettes and 'henna ladies' until the dinner bell rang. Then they put their corn tassel dolls to bed with blankets of dry corn husks – until next year, as it happened – as the corn harvesters came the next day and in all the excitement, the girls forgot about their dolls until the corncrib was full almost to the roof.

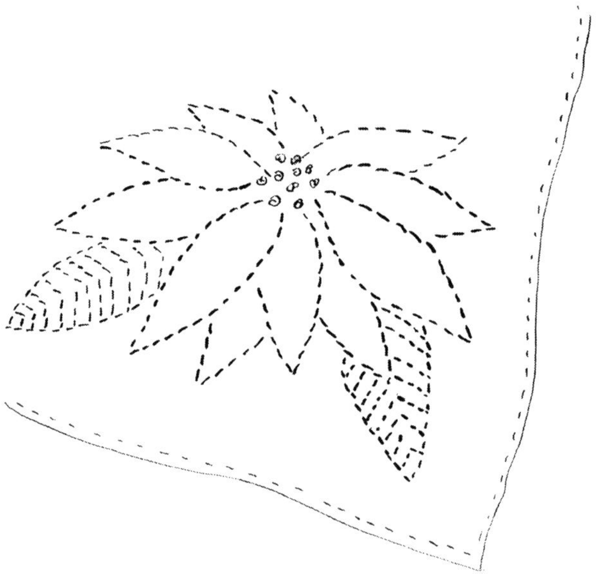

# Poinsettia

Mr. Dalton had come to the porch door, interrupting Bree's game of solitaire. She was annoyed because he had come just before sunset; and that meant Grandma would invite him to stay for supper. Old Mr. Dalton usually came by about once a week – one could never be sure when – but Grandma always said, "Don't matter; he don't have much ta eat anyways, up ta his cabin, an' we got plenty."

Mr. Dalton never said much, except to call his dog, Goodshep, or say, "Good evening."

Even when they all sat at the big round table for dinner, light of the kerosene chimney flickering golden on all the family faces, he sat alone—beyond the light, at a little table that Grandma cleared of magazines and brought into the kitchen. As he sat there, Mr. Dalton's shadow rose on the wall nearly to the ceiling, mimicking him as he ate with a spoon. He never looked up at the family, or asked for salt or another helping of potatoes. Grandma was careful to fill his plate just right before he sat down, because if she leaned over and asked, "Sure you don't want another helping of them green beans?" old Mr. Dalton would shake his head No, never quite looking at Grandma, the whiskery, white bristles around his mouth never twisting into a smile.

Grandma told Bree when she had asked, "He don't want to sit with us, never."

"Well, he sure enough does like eatin' with us," Uncle had said. "Can't blame him much, Ma!"

At the screen door, Mr. Dalton's only greeting was to take off his cap and wait for Grandma to push open the door and say, "Good evening, Mr. Dalton, won't you come in for a bite of supper?"

Goodshep would turn around twice after his tail and lie down outside the screen door, knowing Grandma wouldn't let a dog in. Uncle's dogs never barked at Goodshep, either – just let him be – like the grownups did Old Man Dalton.

Bree had seen his cabin once, when she and Mother and Grandma had picked blackberries. It was a long walk down the road through the pines into a low meadow with cattails, then to higher ground where the blackberry bushes were.

Bree got so hot and thirsty that day (she hated berry picking, anyway) that she had eaten half the berries she picked. The blackberry spines scratched her hands and purple juice ran down her arms.

When they had picked enough buckets of blackberries for making jelly, Grandma said, "Why don't we go see if Old Mr. Dalton's around?"

"He's not much used to visitors, is he?" asked Mother.

"No, he ain't. But he might be glad ta see us; don't suppose nobody much goes there. He just stays ta himself and don't bother nobody."

"He makes you fix up dinner for him every week or so."

"Don't mind. I do dinner anyway."

"Well," said Mother, "it seems strange to me, his living alone so much."

"You know what stories go around. Don't reckon much of them is true. He ain't never done nothing bad—what I know of. And sometimes I wonder, what if he took sick with none of us to know. We do kinda keep check by his coming around once in a while, though what he wants, I think, is company. He just don't know how to make it."

"He can't be as old as you," said Mother.

"Couldn't be nobody so old as me! So old and still love pickin' them berries so! Have, ever since I was a kid."

Bree looked at Grandma. There was no way she could imagine fat, old Grandma with her pink face and curled-up white hair ever being a girl like herself.

"Did you know Dalton in the old days?" Bree's mother asked.

"No," said Grandma. "He came here after the war, World War I. Stories went around then, though they has kinda died out now. Said he brought a French woman back with him after the war, and then she disappeared."

"Well, I always wondered what happened."

"Don't know it was anything more than rumors that happened. But the French woman left."

Bree and her mother and grandmother walked over a field to a row of poplars and entered a sandy lane. Before them was the cabin. In a high, rosy voice, Grandma called, "Mr. Dalton, are you there? Mr. Dalton?"

Bree hoped he wasn't, because in a way he scared her, but it wasn't nice to hope that, she supposed. He wasn't there anyway, so they walked up to the cabin and peeked through the windows. On tip-toe, Bree saw a quilt on a cot, a table and a chair, and a shelf that held a bowl turned upside down. A water dipper hung from the shelf and in front of her on a table was a coffee cup and a copy of *Sportsman*. It had a man on the cover in a red mackinaw with a gun over his shoulder and two geese dangling from his hand. Spread over the table were wires and bits of bright feathers.

"Hey, Grandma, what are those?"

"Fishing flies, Bree. Sure enough, he ain't here. He's

probably gone fishing at Linwood."

Bree had been to Linwood Lake on picnics. She knew it was far because the family always packed up and went in the car. "That's a long way," she said.

"Mr. Dalton don't mind, Bree. He has Goodshep to walk with him. He ain't got nothin' else to do. But we better be gettin' back to fix supper."

They fetched the berry buckets they had left in the shade at the side of the lane and walked back to Grandma's. Bree's hands got tired carrying her bucket, but her bare feet felt wonderfully warm in the soft sand of the road. She looked back at the row of poplars still visible beyond the pines and wondered about Old Dalton and the French woman who disappeared.

Whenever Mr. Dalton came to Grandma's, Bree looked over at him, but he never looked up and left right after supper.

~

Next summer, Bree, Retta, and Dickie were sitting on the barnyard fence wondering what to do when Bree said, "I know!"

"Yeah?" said Dickie, who'd been chewing on barley grains, then spit them out.

"Yeah! I dare everybody to go to Old Man Dalton's!"

"What if he's there?"

"Don't matter."

"You can't just go walking into his place."

"Why not?"

"...'cause nobody goes walking into his place, that's why."

"Why not?" said Bree. "I've been there once—last year!"

"Don't wanna," said Dickie.

"You're just scared, that's what!"

"No, I ain't!"

"Okay, let's go then," said Retta. "He ain't done nothin' bad—what I know of."

"Made some French lady disappear," said Dickie.

"Least we can see if he's 'round the place."

"He won't scare us away, I betcha."

"We can't tell nobody where we're going."

"Let's just say we're going on a picnic."

"Let's be hobos, carry lunch wrapped up."

"Bring some cookies."

"Okay, come on!"

Grandma wasn't in the kitchen standing over the stove. She wasn't anywhere.

"She's probably in the you-know-where," said Retta. Bree tried to erase *that* picture of Grandma from her mind. She had never told her cousins how she'd surprised Grandma there.

"Think we could take some food anyway?" asked Bree.

"Sure," said Retta. "Grandma'd give it ta us if she was here, wouldn't she?" They took sugar cookies from a big glass jar in the pantry, handfuls of raisins, and the last crackers from a box.

Bree grabbed a dishtowel and spread it out.

"Hey," said Retta, "we shouldn't use that one. See the

poinsettia? Peg sewed that for Grandma for Christmas."

Bree pulled the embroidered corner of the towel nearer. "That's pretty nice."

"Don't matter," said Dickie. "We'll bring it right back after the picnic."

They put the goodies in the dishtowel, each vowing to carry the knapsack partway.

"Better leave a note so nobody gets suspicious." Bree tore off a strip of Sears catalogue and wrote 'On Picnic' then grabbed the knotted corners of Peg's poinsettia dishtowel.

The hike was farther than Bree remembered. She had to think hard where to turn off the road, but the row of poplar trees was visible, right where she thought it ought to be.

"See, I told you I knew where it was, didn't I?"

At the edge of the clearing, with Old Man Dalton's place in sight, she said, "We've got to see if he's home or not." She called, "Mr. Dalton?"

Then they all yelled. Assured he was not there after all, Bree said, "Come on, let's look. Scaredy cats!"

"No, we ain't," said Dickie. "Come on, he ain't here."

"Maybe he might come back and find us peekin' in," said Retta.

"So what? All ya gotta do is say, 'Hello, Mr. Dalton, howerya?' "

"Well, if we see 'im comin' and he don't see us—let's run!"

"But quiet-like!"

"Yeah, shut up! Let's peek in."

The cabin was as Bree remembered: a small shed of wood siding, one dark window facing them like an eye looking out, guarding the secrets of Old Man Dalton. Bree shaded her eyes from the sunlight to better look in.

"See somethin'?"

"Naw—do you?"

"Don't see much," said Bree. The wooden table looked the same, but the cover of *Sportsman* had a fisherman with his fishing rod. A coffee cup had spilled over, staining a corner of the magazine. Otherwise, the place seemed the same – deserted – but the old man's boots were on the floor.

Dickie and Retta were on the other side of the cabin. Their heads were dark against a window. "Bree!" they shouted. "Look there!"

"Where?" What did they mean?

"Can ya see anything?"

The two of them came running around the cabin."Bree!"

"Shuuu, shut up, Dickie!" said Retta. "Don't let him see ya, Bree."

"Old Mr. Dalton? But he's not here!"

"Yes, he is!" She pointed, "See 'im?"

"No," said Bree in the faintest whisper, scared now.

"Well, he's sleepin' in front of your nose!"

"You sure?"

Dickie stretched up as much as he could. "He's right there on the cot and ya can't see 'im?"

Bree looked in again. A form was on the cot—Old Dalton curled up like a cat. "He's just sleeping," she said.

"Drunk," said Retta.

"Dead drunk," said Dickie.

"He ain't dead is he?" They looked at each other.

"Dunno."

"Could be."

"See him breathing any?"

"Nope."

Bree got shivery, just to think that Mr. Dalton was dead. She felt sad all of a sudden, remembering how she had been annoyed when he came to Grandma's door, just because he had interrupted her game of solitaire. But it wouldn't have been polite to go on playing, and now she was glad she hadn't, even if he didn't notice. She should have tried to talk to him, anyway. He wasn't such a bad old guy. Maybe she could have asked about the disappeared lady.

"What should we do?" asked Dickie.

"How do I know?" said Retta. "What do you do about dead people?"

"Bury 'um," said Dickie.

"Suppose we should try the door?" Bree asked.

"Better," said Retta. "You try it, Dickie."

Dickie took a deep breath and disappeared around the corner of the cabin.

The girls heard the doorknob turn back and forth. Was the door locked?

"Nobody ever locks his door around here," said Bree.

"But he *was* kinda funny, though," said Retta. "Not like you laugh at him, but funny."

"Yeah," said Bree. "He was a sad old man."

Dickie rapped on the door. The girls looked through the window into the cabin, into the mystery of Old Mr. Dalton.

"Old Dead Dalton!" exclaimed Retta.

"Isn't nice to say that!"

"Well, he is, ain't..." Retta had no chance to finish. Before their eyes a figure rose up dreamlike – with arms outstretched – a shadow figure that walked to the door.

Retta grabbed Bree by the arm and they tore away fast as they could from the old man's cabin, heading to the closest stand of pines.

"Where's Dickie?!" asked Retta, alarmed and out of breath.

"He's sure running away, too."

"You seen him?"

"No."

"Well, maybe Old Dead Man Dalton's got him!"

"Naw," said Bree. "Dickie can run plenty fast and the old man can't."

"Howdya know?"

The girls came onto the road, still running.

"Wouldn't hurt him anyway."

"Well, maybe..." said Retta. "Hey, ain't that Dickie up ahead?"

"Hey, Dickie," they shouted and ran as fast as they could to catch up. "What happened?"

"I dunno," he said, breathing heavily. "All I know is – soon as I heard a key turning in the lock – I got outta there fast. I wasn't waitin' ta see no dead man open up the door!"

"Howdya know?"

"Gee whiz," said Dickie, "then who was turning the door

handle besides me?"

On they ran, stopping only for breath, running all the way to Grandma's house. At the screen door, Retta whispered, "Where's the picnic stuff?"

"Musta dropped it," said Dickie. The cousins vowed secrecy of the picnic.

At supper, Bree tried to eat. She half expected one of the grownups at the table to ask of their adventure. But talk was very much as usual—boring. At a lull in the conversation, Bree asked, in the calmest voice possible, "What ever happened to Mr. Dalton's dog?"

"Poor old Goodshep finally died last winter," said Grandma. The cousins burst into nervous laughter. Bree saw from the look of the adults, as they raised their heads from their dinner plates, that they didn't understand kids at all.

~

Within the week, Mr. Dalton arrived at the door once again at dinnertime. He sat at the far corner of the kitchen at the little square table and was unusually slow with his dinner.

When Bree had finished her turn helping Grandma with the last of the after-dinner cleanup, and Grandma had just lifted the blazing lantern to carry it into the living room where the others were listening to the radio, Bree looked over at Mr. Dalton.

He pulled a package from his shirt, unwrapped it, and placed Peg's poinsettia dishtowel on a rack by the stove. He glanced over at Bree and the faintest smile crossed his whiskery lips.

She knew, then, that he thought they had left the picnic on the doorstep for him.

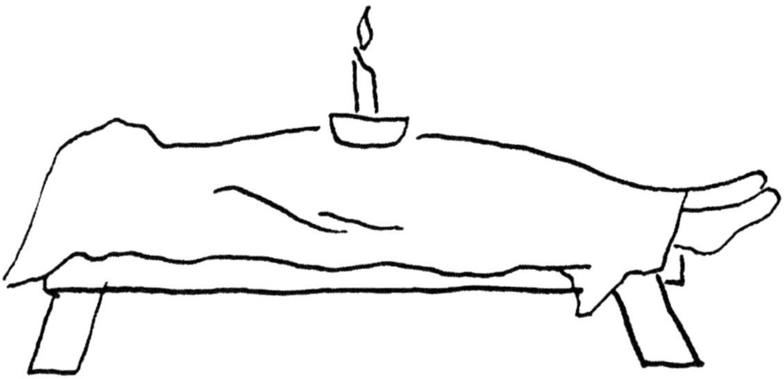

# Pokeweed

An ugly patch of pokeweed grew by the storm cellar door. Nobody liked pokeweed except for a few birds that could eat the purple berries without dying of poison. If there was any really bad plant, Bree thought, *that* was it. Even the leaves were uninteresting. All plants had so many chances of people liking them because of patterns in the leaves or flowers, but pokeweed had nothing pretty about it at all.

It grew by the storm cellar that was dug half into the ground at the far side of the yard. With effort, Bree tugged at the slanting cellar door until it fell open, knocking pokeweeds down. Dickie and Retta had left her to open the door while they went in search of candles and forbidden matches. Bree wondered what her cousins were up to this time.

Last night, everyone had gone into the cellar because of a storm. She'd watched black clouds chase each other across the sky toward the farm, the wind coming up big, bending trees. "Cyclone!" Mother had shouted, and when the storm picked up good, the whole family figured she was right and they went into the storm cellar.

Bree hunkered uncomfortably on a bench and buttoned her sweater. Mother sat next to her. Her cousins poked each other whenever there was a rumble of thunder. Everyone grew solemn when – even under the earth that covered the cellar – winds came like organ blasts. Shattering crashes of lightning strikes, howling winds rising in crescendo, and rain so strong that slivers crawled under the door.

Benches had been pulled from the wall and candles placed on an orange crate in the middle of the cellar. She stared at the flames. There wasn't much else to do. Everyone was quiet except Grandma, who said, "Shame I had to put the fire out on that stew! Everybody's going to get hungry!"

Bree felt too scared to be hungry. Her cousins, looking to her like pale ghosts, watched the flickering candles. Grandma's fleshy body wavered in the candlelight. She seemed to take up more space than anybody else, propping herself up on the bench with her hands on her knees. Bree felt shrunken, like Alice.

"Haven't come down here for a storm in a couple of years," said Grandma. "Course, we store vegetables down here sometimes, but we don't hardly get no use out of the storm cellar, 'cept in times like this—thank goodness! Ain't pleasant down here."

Bree shivered as a crack of lightning seemed to raise the bench right up from the floor.

"Kinda looks like a good storm, too!" said Grandma. "Nothing like the old days, though. I remember when Old Man Richardson found his cow two days after, hung up on a tree about a half mile on down the road. You children might not be believing it much, but I seen for myself a shaft of hay blown right through the trunk of a tree. Wedged so tight, there was no way of pulling it out. Now what do you say to that?"

Before anyone could say anything, a rip of thunder and a crash of something falling right outside the cellar made the cousins duck their heads. "Lightning must have hit that big elm," said Uncle.

After what seemed hours, when the wind stopped blowing and the rain calmed, Uncle pushed back the big door of the cellar and they crawled out. The sky was a spooky red color that Bree had never seen before.

“It’s so quiet, like as if the earth won’t wake up again,” said Grandma. But rain was still falling from tree branches and gutters on the house. Underfoot, the ground had turned to mush.

“Well,” said Grandma, “will you look over there!”

Bree saw the old tree overturned, its roots twisted, branches cracked apart. She shivered, seeing the damage a storm could do.

Uncle said, “I knew I’d get some firewood out of that old elm, someday. Kinda a shame to see her go, though! That tree must’ve stood here before your pa built the old house, Ma.”

“Yes,” said Grandma. “Remember seeing it here as a girl. We’d been out in the buggy for a long way and when we got back, I had to *go* bad—just couldn’t wait, but somebody had jumped off the buggy ahead of me and got there first. I undid my bonnet – it had beautiful, blue ribbon ties – and I hung it on a branch of that elm and headed into the pine woods quick as I could. Well, when I got back – couldn’t have been long – the bonnet was gone, and I was sick. I begged my brothers if they knew where it was to tell me. But wouldn’t one of them say. I grieved over that bonnet a whole week and then one day I was sent out to the garden, as the boys was late with haying, so I had to go out there – and lo and behold – when I came back, there in that tree was the bonnet, nicely tied by the blue ribbons.”

“I reckon that elm tree was here when your great granddad first settled the farm,” she said, looking over at the cousins, “and that’s been over seventy years.”

“Surprising that tree didn’t go down in the storm of ’32,” said Uncle.

“That was a whopper,” answered Grandma, “the year the

old man over on Linwood Lake grabbed onto a tree in the worst of the storm and got his arms pulled right outta the sockets. Don't think he was ever quite right since."

"Never could do farm work good, after that," said Uncle.

"Well, I better get myself to work and get a fire going on that stew," said Grandma, "but, would you look at that!" Grandma's small flower bed looked like a broom had swept it away. "And that old pokeweed stands there as if nothin' happened."

~

The morning after the big storm, Bree watched her cousins hop across the yard where branches and leaves had fallen into rain puddles, making untidy patches on the soggy grass. Retta and Dickie had found more candles and a sheet. When Retta got to the cellar, she opened her palm, revealing a packet of matches.

"Shhh!" said Retta, closing her fist.

Morning sun streamed into the open cellar door, brightening the dreariness, though the musty smell and puddles were still on the cement floor. "Kinda spooky in here," said Bree.

"Just right for what we're gonna do," said Dickie. "Ghosts! Thought of it last night while we was in here."

"Perfect!" said Retta.

"Kinda smelly, if you ask me," said Bree, "but that's okay."

Retta and Dickie pulled one of the benches into the middle of the cellar. Retta laid down on the bench, adjusting herself. The bench was not long enough.

"I gotta put my knees up."

"That would ruin how ya look!" said Dickie.

"Then you look, Bree!" Retta pulled the sheet over her head and bent her knees. "What da ya think?"

"Better keep your knees down."

"Try this," said Dickie. He placed a candle in a holder on Retta's stomach.

"Are you going to light that candle?" asked Bree.

"Sure," said Dickie. He scratched a match against the match cover. "Don't work!" He tried again. The match flamed. Holding it by the tips of his fingers, he tried a shaky trip to the candle that was on Retta's stomach. "Ouch! Gee!" Dickie dropped the match.

"Better step on it," said Bree.

"I can't do it any faster!"

"I mean put the match out. Step on it."

"Who's got shoes?"

Bree was standing in a puddle barefoot, the burnt out match not far from her big toe. "You ought to bring the candle to the door," said Bree. "Then you can see the wick."

"Hurry up, why don'cha?" said Retta from under the sheet. "I can't breathe under here... 'sides, the bench is biting my ankles."

Dickie struck a third match and lit the candle. "Those matches sure do stink," he said, "but close the door, anyway, Bree. Can't have light in here, not with this candle."

He placed the candle on Retta's stomach. "Okay?"

"Yeah, okay, but how am I supposed to rise up? Ain't that what ghosts do?"

"Go on, Bree, shut the door!"

“But it’s pretty heavy, Dickie. What if we can’t get it open again?”

“Go on!”

Bree ducked her head just as the door slammed shut over her.

“That’s better,” said Dickie. “Hocus Pocus, Fee Fi Fo Fum, I smell the blood...” He sputtered in a cough.

“It’s the matches,” said Bree. “They’re terrible. I can’t stand it anymore!”

“Let me outta here!” cried Retta from under the sheet.

“Let me finish the ritchal first,” said Dickie.

“Take that candle off me!”

“In a minute—jus’ wait!”

“Gee, Dickie!” said Retta.

“Abracadabra, Fee Fi Fo Fum!” Bree and Dickie stared at the candle flame on Retta’s stomach.

“I thought I saw the candle rise up, then go down again. Hey Retta, is that you?” said Dickie.

“Sure, it’s me—who da ya think?” said Retta in a choked voice.

“Hey, there it goes again. See it rise up!”

“Get that candle off me,” shouted Retta. “I gotta get out of here! I gotta...”

As Bree lifted the candle, Retta rose up and let out a huge sneeze, then another. “Geez,” she said, “those matches are terrible! Let’s get out of here!”

Bree went to the door. She tried to push it up, but the door wouldn’t budge. “Do you think it’s too heavy—to ever…?”

“Let me try!” said Dickie. Bree thought to herself, he thinks he can do everything. Retta, still wrapped in the sheet, was doubled over in a fit of sneezing.

“Come on,” said Dickie, “we all gotta try together.”

“It’s a lot harder lifting something up over your head,” said Bree. “Gravity is against you.”

“Who is?” asked Retta.

“Somebody up there on the outside holding the door down, do you suppose?” asked Dickie.

“Peg, maybe?” asked Retta.

“Hey, Peg! Peggy!” they cried.

“She wouldn’t let us know if she was there, anyway, would she?” said Retta. “She’d just sit on top of the door reading a book or somethin’.”

“What if we’re caught in here?” asked Bree. “Wouldn’t they come looking for us?”

“Peg already knows where we are—if she’s sitting up there.”

“What should we do?”

“Guess we could be here a long time,” said Retta.

“Why don’t we try abracadabra, again?” said Bree. She meant it halfway as a joke.

Dickie said, “Alright,” and raised his hands to the door overhead. In unison they said, “Abracadabra, open sesame!”

Nothing happened. “Let’s try her again,” said Dickie.

“Aw, nothin’ will happen,” said Retta.

“Might,” said Dickie. “Let’s try it once more, but this time everybody push up hard on ‘open’!”

“Abracadabra!” they yelled. “Abracadabra op...!” The door flung open and they flew right out.

“Wow!” said Dickie. “Sure worked!”

“Yeah!” said Retta.

But Bree caught sight of Mother trying to get up from the tangle of pokeweed by the door.

“Heavens!” said Mother. “I thought I heard something in there—didn’t know it was a cyclone! What are you children up to?!”

“Nothin’!”

“Yeh, nothing!”

# Lilacs

Bree had been waiting weeks for the first day of May that promised so much – one of the best days of the year – but the sky overhead was distressingly grey when she wished for sunshine. Rain would be a disaster for crepe paper. Still, she could hope that the licks of wind on her rain slicker and the few drops already falling would have it out and be gone before May basket time.

She better walk faster to school. She'd started late, looking once again at the violet, pink, yellow, and green baskets on the dining table. She had helped Mother make them from match boxes, cheese cartons, and paper cups. They were disguised by frilled, colored crepe paper gathered in layers, then sewn and glued. Bree braided the crepe paper handles herself, and Mother stapled them.

Bree looked at the baskets this morning, regretting a little, to give them away – they were so pretty – yet she was happy that the first day of May finally had come. She could fill the baskets with mints, popcorn, and chocolate kisses and top each one with a spray of lilac.

She checked, shoes wet in the grass, before cutting through the alley to school. Although the white and purple buds were not ready, the violet-colored lilacs were perfect.

Thinking of May baskets, it wasn't until Bree slid into her desk at the sound of the school bell that she thought of the ordeal to be faced. There was no way to escape what she already knew would be humiliation. Her costume had hung so loosely on her at rehearsal yesterday that she felt just what Mother said, "So awkward!"

Why was *she* chosen for the Maypole dance? She didn't know how eight girls, including, thank goodness, Betty from her own fourth grade class, would get through the dance without crossing the colored streamers into a wrong-way tangle. The dancers were to pass left shoulder to left, then right to right, winding green and pink streamers from opposite directions around the Maypole.

Her teacher, Mrs. Pickrell, had explained the festivities of May, which was the reason they were doing the dance at all. Bree hoped to be so lucky that rain would call off the program; yet, above all, she wanted the weather to be fine for May baskets.

Outside the classroom windows the sky was dark, and there was lightning far off. Inside, the class had another grueling half-hour of social studies before she would have to go down to the basement to put on her costume. But Mrs. Pickrell was making an announcement. "The May Day celebrations will not take place" – Bree held her breath – "on the school grounds, but in the gymnasium."

That was an even gloomier prospect with everyone crowding in close to the dancers.

"Children! Children!" Mrs. Pickrell shouted. The class was agitated. Bree tried to form a connection in her mind between the flashes of lightning outside, the Maypole dance, and her beautiful May baskets. But Mrs. Pickrell was saying, "Let's go back to a few things we said yesterday. Who knows…," she asked in a big voice, then quieted right down again in the way teachers do, so you can't hear them at all unless you listen carefully, "…who is the goddess of May?"

There was silence in the room. "Don't you remember? The goddess Maia." She spelt it out on the board. M-a-i-a. "And Ceres, C-e-r-e-s, is the goddess of growing things, especially the plants we eat."

Bree heard her say something about gathering flowers of spring. And what seemed ages later, she and Betty were dismissed to the girls' room in the basement to change into their costumes.

The Maypole dance was the third selection from the last on the program. The principal gave the welcome after *The Pledge of Allegiance* "...with liberty and justice for all."

Bree stood in her costume, waiting to do something she didn't want to do, and she wondered about the justice of *that.* Mrs. Pickrell talked about Health Day and drinking milk and eating vegetables, but for Bree, the first day of May would always mean May baskets.

Finally, the chorus sang *My Country 'Tis of Thee*, then the piano tinkling *Glowworm* signaled the start of the Maypole dance. Mrs. Pickrell was playing up and down the keyboard with curlicues and fancy runs, until it was hard for Bree to hear where the music was, until Mrs. Pickrell turned her head and loudly whispered, "Now!"

The difficulty for Bree was in keeping her streamer winding in and out around the others to the beat of the music. Either she had to rush ahead to meet the next dancer or barely move. Bree prayed to be out of the badly twisted streamers when a bolt of lightning struck electric sparks right before her eyes. The room seemed to explode, then shrink back from a tremendous crack of thunder. A moment passed before everyone in the gymnasium came back to their senses.

Had her prayer been answered? The Maypole was in such disarray that Mrs. Pickrell suggested they move on, singing *America the Beautiful.* Bree ran off the floor to the girls' bathroom. "Whew," said Betty, who was already there. "I thought we'd never get through that!"

"We didn't," said Bree. "It was awful!"

"What time are you going out with May baskets?" Betty asked.

"About five."

"Me, too. Maybe I'll see you."

Bree now prayed for the sun to come out. "Sunshine, dry my lilacs. Rain, please don't cry on my pretty baskets!"

As soon as the 3:10 bell rang, Bree ran home. She filled the baskets with candies and picked the daintiest sprays of lilac. She chose the most beautiful baskets for the most special people. Here, her heart got tied up—her girlfriends, and the new boy from Illinois. She wanted to give him the best basket. She selected one that had three colors of crepe paper braid on the handle. Bree took an extra foil-wrapped chocolate kiss from another basket and put it in his.

May baskets were a game. Sneaking onto a porch, she'd ring the doorbell, leave the basket, and run away as fast as she could. She would hide by the side of the house or behind a tree. Sometimes someone would open the door and catch her, and with shouts and screams, she'd get caught and get a hug or a kiss.

Bree was near *his* house, the boy from Illinois. She remembered every conversation with him since the first day he had come to school.

"Do you have roller-skates?" she asked.

"Yeah!"

"I skate Saturdays by the church."

"Have a bike?"

"Nope. But let's go..."

They never roller-skated together to the ice cream store

down the street from her house, but Bree wished they would. You could get three different kinds of ice cream in a double cone for a nickel. She approached the house, hoping he was there – then couldn't believe her eyes – Betty was coming down the sidewalk from the opposite direction with a basket on her arm.

"What are *you* doing here?"

"You like him? Me, too."

The girls put their May baskets down together. Betty rang the doorbell and they ran down the steps to the far side of a big lilac bush, its limbs drooping with armfuls of lilacs. Bree thought they were the sweetest smelling flowers in the world. She drew a deep breath.

"Scared he will find us?" asked Betty.

"No." Bree hoped he would.

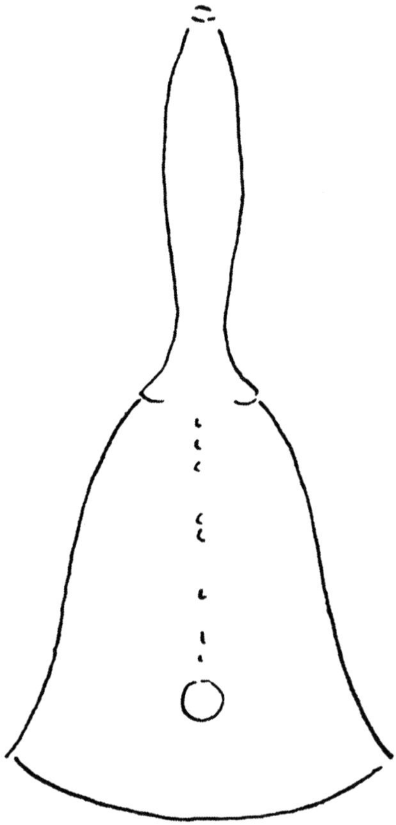

# The Bluebell

There were seventy-nine of them in the dim light. Bree could reach up on the dining room sideboard and touch certain bells cautiously, but only a few. The bells waited for her to come, waited for her touch and the movement of her arm to bring their sounds alive, to change the dark silence into song.

There were bells over the fireplace mantel and on bookshelves, the books removed and piled on the floor or out in the hallway by the stairs, all to make room for the bells. The bells on the sideboard were there for her to play when she came to visit.

It would occur to her to visit the bells and Mrs. Rising when she passed the old white house on the corner, with its windows closed and curtains pulled, even on a sunny spring Saturday. Speeding by on her new bike, Bree heard the bells in her ears and thought of poor Mrs. Rising lying there while she was free to go riding right by and never turn back, to pedal on around the corner past the Methodist church and rounding the next corner, be home.

But something shimmered as she passed the house. Was it the noontime sunlight through the leaves of the huge, dark elms? Something stopped Bree. She got off and walked her bike back to the porch steps. She hunted in the yard for something sweet, a bouquet for Mrs. Rising, but found only crabgrass, so she came empty-handed to the door and knocked as hard as she could.

Mother had told her always to knock first and then let herself in. She closed the door and listened. In the living room, there was the sound of a bedsheet crumpling and then Mrs. Rising's thin voice, "Bree, is that you? Yes, I know it is you. I can tell by that knock. Come in, girl!"

Bree could hardly speak as she stood in the darkness before Mrs. Rising. It always happened like that. She would get up her courage, then words fled and she couldn't remember anything to say to fill the silence.

Mrs. Rising was there in the living room, as always, elevated on a high bed, her head slightly raised, a sheet falling over her as if she were floating in space. "Levitating," her father had said, "like the Fakirs of India who can levitate through sheer force of will over matter. A state of mind that we Westerners are as yet unable to attain."

It wasn't Mrs. Rising's mind that kept her in the air; it was the high bed that Bree sometimes was allowed to adjust, though Mrs. Rising never did sit up, as far as Bree knew. It was not her mind that kept her down, but her sickness.

"Well, what have you been doing today, Bree?" she asked.

"Riding my bike."

"And what did you see?"

"The elm tree leaves out front and sunlight coming through them."

"And the grass?"

"Green by the porch."

"Crabgrass?"

"Yes."

"Well, it's the hardy kind that takes over. Has to be tough for the Nebraska weather. But it is almost summer. How many days until school is out, Bree?"

"Thirteen."

"I knew you could tell me."

All this time, Bree had been unable to look around for the bells. She couldn't take her eyes, in gloomy fascination, from Mrs. Rising's face. She looked very old—her face bluish in the pale light, the skin smooth but sagging over her cheeks, her small mouth puckered, like Bree's when she sucked a lemon.

Bree was able to stare into the dark pools of Mrs. Rising's sunken eyes – once she knew – once Mother had definitely said that Mrs. Rising could not see at all. To know that made Bree sad. But Father said there were many ways to 'see' other than with one's eyes – by touch, by sound – and Bree had experimented with her eyes closed, tripping on a street curb, hitting her shin. She had tried for seconds to ride her bike with her eyes closed, but she was afraid of a smash-up. She had smelled the elm trees and tried to hear ants busy at an anthill. And she would have to put her mind to it harder, when she went into her bedroom closet and tried drawing horses in the dark.

"Bree, would you like to play the bells?"

Bree hoped that Mrs. Rising, in that other way her father talked of, 'the sixth sense,' couldn't see that the bells were the reason Bree came. They had a game. Bree would ring a bell, and then ask Mrs. Rising which bell it was. Mrs. Rising always knew, just from the sound, which bell Bree held in her hand.

She had gifts of bells from all around the world: one from a bishop in England, and an Indian sent her an antique brass bell from India where the Fakirs live. Bree's father had joked about the 'Fakirs' and the 'fakers' and told her the difference, even though the words sound the same.

It was some time before Bree had understood that although Mrs. Rising memorized the sounds of bells, she had never seen them.

"Are they all there on the sideboard, Bree?"

"Yes, Mrs. Rising."

The bells were set on a crocheted runner: fat ones squatting, some heavy in her hand and not as pretty, but able to make the biggest or best sounds. Others were light in sound and graceful. The bells were like people, each sounding a little different, looking a little different from the other.

Mrs. Rising sent her into the dark interior, searching cupboards, shelves, or the fireplace mantel for a certain bell. "Do you see it, Bree, the bell with a picture of Salisbury Cathedral? Have you heard of that?"

"No, Mrs. Rising."

"Salisbury is one of the most beautiful cathedrals in the world. Far away in England." Bree looked hard in the dull light, but she couldn't see much beautiful in the brownish picture of the cathedral.

"Over to my left, in the glass cabinet – open the door carefully – about in the middle of the shelf is a white china bell with a picture and the words 'Blue Mountains.' A kind man from Australia sent that to me many years ago. Do you know where Australia is?"

"No, but I think it is a long way."

"A very long way. On the other side of the world, 'down under' they say." Bree had a hard time thinking that far. She'd hardly been outside Nebraska, except to visit her cousins in Minnesota.

"Play the bells for me, Bree."

She would surprise Mrs. Rising. She didn't start with a soft bell, as usual, but chose a big school bell with a wooden handle. Clang, clang, clang. Mrs. Rising laughed—something so rare that it startled Bree. "Well, you are adventurous this morning! And even when it is Saturday, you chose the school bell. Then you *do* like school! Even when you tell me differently."

"School's not bad."

"If you learn to read well, Bree, you can learn all about the world in books. I read special books, called Braille. I know words by touch." Bree found one of Mrs. Rising's books and felt the dots with her fingertips.

Maybe that was what Father was talking about—different ways of seeing.

"Now, let's try another bell." Bree chose a slender metal bell that tinkled as soon as she touched it.

"My, that one is high-strung and nervous today," said Mrs. Rising. "Ring that again. That's fine! Now, see if you can imitate that tone with your voice. Just sing with a good breath."

Bree never stopped to think on anything that Mrs. Rising told her to do, so she opened her mouth and out popped a sound.

"Now open inside your throat, keeping your mouth round. Imagine your mouth like the inside of a bell. Sing through the bell with a 'me' sound."

Bree did, and liked the sound.

"Pick up another bell. Ring it and sing out with a big 'Ding'! That's good! Try another bell."

She sang out—"Dong," and felt it ring in her head.

"That's good! You have good pitch. That means you can hear, then make the same tone as the bell." Mrs. Rising faced Bree with those deep eyes. "Do you understand?"

Bree thought she did. She liked to sing, but she was getting anxious to get out into the sun again.

"You have a bell tone in that lovely voice, Bree."

Bree set the last bell carefully back in place. "I think I have to go. It's lunch time."

"It probably is—I don't mind after the hours anymore," said Mrs. Rising.

She is tired, thought Bree. So then I *should* go.

"Bye," she said, happy as she could, though she felt sad.

"Bree, before you go, would you find a certain bell for me?"

"Yes, Mrs. Rising." She was beginning to 'see' that Mrs. Rising used Bree's eyes to place certain bells in mind, to be able to tell her few visitors where those bells were.

"On my right side, on the second shelf of the bookcase, there is a china bell. Do you see it? The one with flowers?"

Bree rarely touched other bells—only the bells she was allowed to play from the sideboard. She held a bell toward a slat of light near a drawn window shade. "I see blue flowers on it."

"Those are harebells," Mrs. Rising said. "We call them bluebells. See how each flower grows up from the stem, each flower like a bell? Play it!"

Bree gave the bluebell bell a cautious shake.

"No, ring it, Bree, a little louder. A bit more, now."

Bree rang the bell gently, then firmly until the tone, high and clear, rang through the room, vibrating through her body.

"Alright! That is enough, Bree!" said Mrs. Rising, smiling.

“Remember that sound: not loud, or brash, or overwhelming. Not shy and unassertive, either. Firm and gentle. That is how the bell should sound. Do you understand?”

Bree nodded her head, though she really didn’t understand, lost as she was in a remembered ringing of the bell. It then occurred to her that Mrs. Rising couldn’t see her nod her head, so she said, “Yes, Mrs. Rising.”

“That bell belonged to my grandmother. I remember hearing that from the time I was a little girl. I want you to have the bell. Take it Bree—to remember what I have said.”

Bree was so surprised that she could not think of anything to say.

“Are you going, then?” asked Mrs. Rising.

Bree looked at the shadow form floating there in the room with the bells. “Yes, Mrs. Rising. And thank you!”

It was impossible to ride her bike and carry the bell carefully at the same time, so Bree walked home. She would have to find a good place to keep the bell to remember—to remember what?

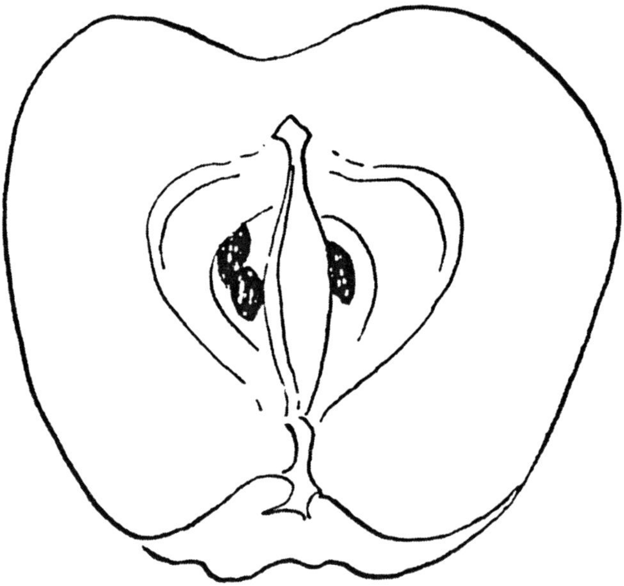

# Seeds of the Apple

If she counted desks in the classroom, there were 32. If she counted desks occupied by listening bodies, that was something *else* altogether. (*Else* follows the word modified.) She had just looked up that word in Webster's Unabridged when her eye caught *elude* (to escape; to evade; to avoid by artifice, stratagem, wiles, deceit, or dexterity; as to elude an enemy; to elude the sight; to elude detection). But where was something she could pin her mind to in this always awful time between spelling and recess?

She saw the apple that had been on Miss Barnes' desk for two days. Teachers had apples in songs and valentines, but this big Red Delicious had tortured her tummy, particularly yesterday during the last ten minutes before lunch. Bree stabbed a pencil into a clean sheet of lined paper. She didn't succeed in breaking the pencil point. That would have been an excuse to go to the pencil sharpener. She began to write *else, else, else*, trying to write each one the same, but they looked else-wise each time—the word loosening, like a cat unwinding a ball of yarn. She would change *else*, capitalize it, making the word important by a stroke of her pencil, changing the word to Elsie, Elsa, Elisa.

She glanced at Betty, who sat behind her in the next row of desks. Miss Barnes had *eluded* Bree, coming from the back of the classroom just as Bree had handed a drawing to Betty.

"Alright, Bree, what is *that* you're doing?"

Bree's hand and a drawing were on Betty's desk. "Drawing."

"Drawing what?"

"Paper dolls."

"Is this the time to do that, do you think?" The class giggled.

"No, Miss Barnes." Any possible explanation eluded Bree at that moment. She had finished her spelling list and was bored writing the same old words over and over.

Penmanship made her hand stiff. A tight hand was the worst thing for drawing. And if she needed to write out words, why not give them character—give herself pleasure in making the swirls, the dotted *i*'s, the double-crossed *t*'s? But she knew that fancy penmanship was not the way to get an A on an essay. In fact, she had almost failed with a C–. She was not sure if a D+ wouldn't be better than a C– but the whole thing had made her miserable.

In her essay, "The Valuable Service of Dogs in the War Effort," she had felt good about the writing, turning it in before the deadline. But Miss Barnes had written on top in red pen, "Please apply penmanship to your essay!"

She wrote it again, not changing any words, only the looks, and got a B. She considered B meant better than bad. She wanted to get an A. But always doing what Miss Barnes wanted – expected her to do – eluded Bree. Her hand slipped into drawing faces for Elsie, Elsa, Elisa.

She was trying to locate her colored pencils under the lid of her desk when Miss Barnes asked, "What is that you're doing, Bree?"

"Looking for my colored pencils."

"This is not drawing class," said Miss Barnes, continuing to repeat the list of spelling words for the next day.

Bree sighed. What else could she do for the whole five

minutes until the hands of the clock clicked into position at 10:55 and the recess bell rang?

She found a lead pencil under her desk and drew on a blank piece of paper. At home, she had a special indelible pencil that her father had given her; with a moist finger, she could smear purple color onto a page, could make watery designs, yet the first line would never wash away. There must be indelible lines like that in her brain. Things she wouldn't forget.

The bell rang. Finally, something *else*! This had been one of those mornings—actually they happened pretty often, when she couldn't keep her mind on what was going on in class. She tuned in and out like a radio.

The recess bell jangled her body to action. The boys and girls separated to their own drinking fountains. The boys then went to the soccer field and the girls jumped rope. The swings, to Bree's regret, had been left behind when she passed third grade.

"Hey, Bree!" Betty was calling. She had a jump rope.

"Gee," said Bree, "I don't think I can stand another spelling lesson."

"Me either," said Betty.

"Do you know, is a D+ higher than a C–?"

"Don't know," said Betty, "I don't get them. We'll jump 'til whoever misses, okay?"

"And let's make up the verses," said Bree. "You start."

Betty began, "Jump, jump, try to squash..."

"...the big D-licious of the boss." The rope went round and round, their breath staccatoing the words as they jumped. "Make – tea – cher's – ap – ple – ap – ple – sauce!"

Bree's head went forward just as the rope caught Betty on the back of the legs. Betty pitched forward and struck Bree's nose hard with her head. "Owwww!"

"Ouch!" said Betty. "Did I lose a tooth?"

"Still there," said Bree. "Are you okay?"

"Yeah," said Betty, "but you got a bloody nose!"

"Oh shoot!" said Bree, feeling courageous, fighting back the hurt. "Feels just like when that jerk hit me with a snowball last year. My nose has been crooked ever since." She laughed, and then her voice wavered, close to a breakdown as she felt the pain. She couldn't cry here on the playground with boys looking on.

Now arms were around her shoulders, patting her, consoling her, pushing her toward the nurse's room with "You'll be alright, Bree." "Does it hurt much?" And Betty, taking charge, opened the big, old door, then ran down the hall (running the risk of sitting in the principal's office) to alert the nurse that she, Bree, was wounded. But she was defended by faithful friends, backed up by them, weakened by their sympathy, which now almost made her cry, though the pain was easing away. The girls, excited and so eager to help, told the nurse five or six times what had happened. They were told to go back to the playground.

The nurse stuck a cotton compress under Bree's upper lip and said, "That will stop it!" Then she gently cleaned Bree's face. "Now that the bleeding has stopped, why don't you lie down a moment."

Bree looked at the clock in the nurse's room. Time was into math period. She lay back on the cot. A luxury of moments came over her. She could hear them ticking on the big clock. She closed her eyes, thinking how her faithful friends had come to her aid, like the valiant dogs in her essay came to the aid of soldiers in the war.

"Bree! Come on, wake up!" The nurse was standing over her. "Are you alright?" She pulled up Bree's eyelids with her thumb. "I'll take that compress out of your mouth."

Bree looked up at the clock. Ten minutes after 12:00. The bell would ring. She'd done it—completely *eluded* math class!

# Poppies

The world outside Nebraska came to Bree each evening when her father listened to the radio and Elmer Davis announced the news of the war. World War II was too far away for her to imagine what it was like, except for air raid drills when civil defense sirens wailed, and she had to pull down the window shades and stay inside, or when the boy next door buzzed low in a P-38 and her house shook. Of course, he wasn't dropping bombs on them, only the enemy. The boy who had cut their grass in summer and shoveled snow in winter, was blown up with the *Arizona* at Pearl Harbor. In Sunday school, she heard of soldiers saved from bullets by New Testament Bibles in their breast pockets.

Bree didn't want to think about war, but when art class came and the teacher put on the gloomy Beethoven record that begins with fate knocking at the door, she had to think about it. In the classroom, knitting needles were clicking in opposition to Beethoven, in a long line for the war effort. Almost everyone was knitting afghan squares, but she had chosen to make a Veteran's Day poster instead.

On Veteran's Day, nice ladies with red crepe paper poppies in their buttonholes and giggly high school girls with donation cups asked everyone to buy a poppy. Bree was painting poppies in a field, like Flanders Field, where – she'd memorized this for English class – "the poppies blow... between the crosses, row on row."

Poppies were symbols for the bodies of soldiers in World War I. Now the poppies were for lost soldiers of the Second World War. Her poster had dimes falling out of the sky, instead of bombs, dimes to buy the poppies and help wounded veterans.

She brought from home her own tube of blue paint that her father had given her for her 11th birthday. Cerulean was a strong blue that tore open the color of the poppies, like blood.

When the teacher replaced Beethoven with the *Warsaw Concerto*, Bree looked up from the poster. Kids were bent over their yarn, needles clicking, the music turned up too loud to talk while they knit for the soldiers. If she were there, somewhere across the oceans, she would wrap an afghan around a soldier's legs, or his one leg. She felt sad to think of those poor soldiers and there was nothing she could do to stop the arms and legs getting blasted off, but sit in art class and paint a poster.

She did collect metal hangers, a wagonload full, that were made into guns for the soldiers. She saved tin cans and smashed them flat. All the kids saved gum wrapper foil and rolled it into balls that got as big as baseballs. When she had nothing better to do, she tacked pictures of Hitler, Tojo, and Mussolini on the garage door and threw mud balls at them.

Sometimes Mother folded bandages in the church basement for the Red Cross. Those days Bree had to sit on the steps in the cold, waiting for Mother to come home. She was not to complain, for that was part of her war effort.

And this is, too, she thought, mixing lots of blue paint from the tube with water and smoothing it creamy with her biggest brush. The teacher turned off the music and asked, "Has anyone finished a square?" A lot of boys raised their hands. "Yes," she said, "it looks like the boys have won again this week!"

Contests. Bree guessed that was the way teachers got kids to do anything. She had hopes of winning the Veteran's

Day poster contest. Starting from the top, Bree painted quickly all the way down around the dimes to the poppies before the sky had dried. She made a blue sky reaching to forever, a peaceful sky that touched the poppies and the graves of all the brave soldiers lost.

# The White Rose

It was December 23rd. Snow was everywhere. Falling snowflakes sparkled under streetlights. The night felt cold on her cheek, yet soft as chilled rose petals in a crystal vase of snow. Her breath hung in wreaths, like images of what was spoken after words were gone, words which just then were, "Stop it, Craig!"

He stood behind her, kicking at the heels of her galoshes, shattering her beautiful moment. But she had seen one crystal snowflake reflected in the light and knew that she could keep it forever in her mind, knew that other beautiful things would fall to her like gifts, expected or surprise, given especially to her if she opened her eyes to see in a special way.

"Cut it out, Craig!" He was holding the ends of her scarf, pulling it tight around her neck.

The boys and girls tramped down the dark street in woolens and leggings, caps and earmuffs, laughing, stumbling toward those ahead of them in the snow. As they walked a shoveled path or climbed snow piles, they held on to each other in rows. Girls clung to girls like cut-out paper dolls. Boys slid on ice and stomped on ice bubbles in the street until they made sharp, hollow crackling.

"Alright, boys and girls, here we are. Pay attention now!" Mr. Grant was trying to get the fifth and sixth graders together for carol singing.

Craig punched her. "Hey, Bree, you know the words?"

"Of course I know the words!"

The carolers started out weakly with *O Come, All Ye Faithful*, even after Mr. Grant's instruction on how to attack; that was what he said, 'attack' the first word of the song. Now the carolers were gaining strength, getting used to the rush of cold air in their lungs.

A door opened, and Mr. Brown looked out at them, and then came his wife, who wore a leg brace, and leaned against the door for support.

Bree felt the power of her breath to sing a whole line without running out of sound when she got to the last word in a phrase, like "O come ye, o co-um ye, to Be-eth-le-hem." Her high notes soared over everyone in *Joy to the World*, when she came to the "Let every heart prepare Him room."

Mr. Brown stood there unable to say a word when they finished, but Mrs. Brown said, "Thank you, children, for taking the trouble to walk over here in the snow to sing so nice for Mr. Brown and me."

Singing *Silent Night* as they left, Bree's voice floated over the carolers in a soft obbligato on the final "Sleep in heavenly peace."

She felt a thud on her back. Snow caught between her neck and coat collar. She turned, exasperated. "Stop it!"

Suddenly, a chorus of snowballs greeted her. "Bree, busy bee. Snow snob! Snow slob!"

The girls called out, "Mr. Grant, Mr. Grant, make the boys stop!" But the music teacher was already at the door of the oldest man in the neighborhood. "At 93," said Mr. Grant, "he's seen more Christmases than anyone around!"

"Well," said Mr. Cole, "if you children don't make a pretty sight to an old man's eyes! Now let me hear you sing as pretty!"

They sang *Good King Wenceslas* for him. Bent over and

beardless, Mr. Cole couldn't have looked less like a king.

"...when the snow lay 'round about

deep and crisp and even...

Brightly shown the moon that night..."

Bree felt as if her toes had turned to ice and might crack right off if she wiggled them, but soon the chorus would go to Mr. Grant's house to stand by a heater and hold cups of hot cocoa to warm their fingers.

The last caroling was at Mrs. Rising's house. As Bree climbed the porch steps, she thought of her bell, her gift from Mrs. Rising.

Mrs. Rising would invite them in like last year, when her husband passed out sugar cookies. The kids had been shy with Mrs. Rising, who, as usual, was suspended on her orthopedic bed, somewhere between a kind of shining joy and her special sadness. Bree knew that Mrs. Rising would be happy just because they came.

But tonight, Mr. Rising stood at the door without greeting them. Mr. Grant said, "The carolers from the elementary school would like to sing some carols for you and Mrs. Rising."

Mr. Rising passed his hand over his eyes as though he were clearing something away so that he could see the children. "I'm sorry," he said, "you see – I'm afraid – Mrs. Rising has taken a turn. We think she won't last..."

Bree was sure she was going to cry. She felt herself melting away into the snow, where she saw in her mind's eye a white rose in crystal drops of snow, petals melting into the snow, snow melting in tears down her cheeks, flowing on to eternity. She didn't know what, but she knew there was a special place for Mrs. Rising, where life would be fair.

Mr. Grant said, “I’m sorry to hear that. Is there anything I can do?”

“No,” said Mr. Rising, “there is nothing to do but wait.”

It seemed impossible that Mrs. Rising wouldn’t be there with her bells and that Bree would never sing for her again.

“Come on, Bree, hurry up!” called her girlfriends.

“Brrr! Aren’t you cold?”

“We’re going to Mr. Grant’s for cocoa and cookies now.”

Bree heard Mrs. Rising’s bells chime in her ears and knew that she would have to suffer this moment alone, that she couldn’t explain. But this moment was one, for good or bad, she would remember always—so many got lost.

# Pine Clearing

Summer sounds came to her—laughter dappling on a breeze, wavelets flowing under her as she lay on her stomach squinting into a dark water world through wooden 2x4s of the dock. She felt that she was drifting, the dock moving farther into the water, journeying where? But motion was in the water. Then black flies lit on her back with a fury that made her jump up and swat the air with a damp towel and pull it hard across her back to rub the itching away.

She heard kids shouting from across the lake, and wished she was there to see who they were. They must be kids from the old stone house that had been on the lake for many years. Her cousins' family cabin, where she was staying now, had been built just a year ago on the developed side of the lake, where small cottages, a boathouse, and a grocery store clung to a dirt roadway that followed halfway around the lake.

The sun momentarily went under a cloud and that made her shiver, drop the towel, and jump into the lake. The water wasn't cold, but it was brown and murky. In the shallows, patches of sun made a strange yellow glow on pebbles underwater. When her feet got tangled in clumps of weeds, she swam to the dock.

Sun spread radiance over her in a blanket of warmth that she could lie into, shielding her eyes, letting the small of her back sink into the planks of the dock. She wondered how she looked, lying there. It was terrible being a girl at her age, especially in a droopy bathing suit. For boys, it didn't matter. But to be a girl! And she wasn't lucky as some, Betty for instance, with her good legs and breasts starting to round nicely. Betty could lie in the sun and get a good tan and not turn splotchy or pimply.

It would be easier to forget all about her body, if she could. Just live from her head up. In school she hated to walk in front of the class to do a math problem—everyone looked at her and then she couldn't concentrate or even think. Mother said that nobody noticed her as much as she *thought* they did, that everybody was only paying attention to themselves, anyway. Bree hoped so. But, by a matter of chance, or bad luck in her case, she had to carry her too tall, too broad-shouldered, flat-chested body around on skinny legs and knobby knees. She had looked through magazines and couldn't help but compare herself to models. Department stores sold clothes for the perfect dummies in the windows.

It was hopeless. She had tried weeks of bumping her bottom against a wall, of stretching her legs like the French can-can girls, and eating nothing but boiled eggs, tomatoes, and grapefruit, but nothing helped. It was sad enough to make her cry, but she would have to live with it, this body of hers that was letting her down. And that other thing was worse, getting the 'curse.' To think of a lifetime of that! "It will make you a woman," Mother said. "You'll have babies someday."

But that was too far away to console her. She would just have to find ways to cheer herself up. Of course, the cousins were coming tonight, and tomorrow—who knows what might happen, what interesting boy might come along. But if he looked at her—disaster! She couldn't pretend. She couldn't make herself better than she was, which, if she looked at herself realistically in a mirror, wasn't terrible. But no one would especially want to be her when she'd seen so many girls she didn't even know, that she immediately would trade places with.

Voices echoed on the water. "Hello, hello, hello!"

She shouted, "Hey, Hey, Hey!" Maybe she'd seen some of the kids at the store or down at the boathouse. An assortment of young and old got thrown together in the summertime. In the winter, at home, the sixth graders (now going into seventh grade) stuck strictly together, closed ranks, and wouldn't let anyone else in. She had had to fight very hard to 'get in' when her parents moved and she had to go to a new school. She had been teased and tested and once, coming home in tears, Mother had said, "Show them their teasing doesn't bother you. Laugh with them and then everything will be alright."

But some of the things she had to do were dumb. Once she had been abandoned in a field in back of the house in a game of hide-and-seek. She could laugh now. She had waited by a clump of bushes for so long, and the kids later swore that they had called her in with "Olly, olly, ox-in-free," but she never heard them.

Another cloud came over the sun. Bree decided that she would go to the cabin and change. Her toes and fingers were wrinkled from soaking in the water.

~

Later, the cousins and her aunt arrived with baskets of food. Bree carried an apple pie to the beach. They were going to picnic by the lake when Uncle finished milking the cows, and drove Grandma over to the cabin.

When last ribbons of sunlight fell on the picnic table and everyone had come, she and Retta and Peg collected dry sticks and built a fire on rocks near the water.

"Bree," said Mother, "run back up to the cabin for catsup and mustard. Hear me now?" They were going to eat hamburgers and pie, and she was already starving before the fire was ready. Darkness would come soon. It would be a good idea to bring a flashlight. Adults often forgot important things like that.

The screen door was ajar, letting mosquitoes in, and they were fierce. Bites swelled quickly on her skin. It was mustard and catsup she'd come for up the path. The fridge light was all she needed in the dark. She slammed the door with her bottom and was ready to head down to the beach when she remembered the flashlight on the table by Mother's bed. Bree felt her way along the edge of the bed. Her fingers touched the cold metal of the flashlight, just as fright knocked the wind out of her. Something crushed her chest. Arms squeezed her, closing so tight on her nipples that they hurt.

"Uggh!" She struggled; maybe Mother's stories of prowlers weren't wrong. Or molesters of girls. She wasn't so much frightened as astonished and wiggled side to side to get free. She put her hands to the vise grip around her and tried to pull the hands loose. She was stronger than she thought, blood pumping into her veins, giving her strength to pry the hands loose. She struggled free and groped for the door. "Who's that?" she exclaimed.

"Shuuu! It's me!"

She knew that voice anywhere. "Dickie, for heaven's sake, what are you doing?"

"Trying ta scare ya, and I did, didn't I?"

"You dumbo, what do you think you're trying to do?"

"Scared ya, didn't I!"

"Well, yeh! What did you expect! But mostly, you just make me mad! For *that*, you can carry down the mustard and catsup that I came up here for. Go on, take them!"

She gave Dickie leeway on the path before she followed him. She was so dumbfounded that she forgot all about the flashlight until she was on the beach. They could all come stumbling up in the dark. The sky was clear, and the moon, she knew, would be almost full. The evening star was up in the bluish grey sky before all the others. She made a wish, as she always did when she saw it, but never told anyone, that her wish was to have a boyfriend someday. If she told anyone, it wouldn't come true.

Hamburgers were cooking over the fire, the adults opening bottles of beer, and the kids were munching potato chips and dill pickles. Mother was spreading butter on buns when she asked, "Did you bring down the catsup and mustard?"

"Yes," said Bree. She wouldn't mention Dickie. That was humiliating, to get caught by a boy, even if he was her own cousin.

After catsup had dripped onto her shirt, and the last hamburger had disappeared and the pie plate was empty, the adults lolled by the fire making dull comments: "Nice day today." "Not too hot." "A few clouds."

Then Grandma said, "I saw Mrs. Pierce at the store today and she says there's going to be a wedding at the lake." Bree tuned her ears up. "A wedding at the old stone house across the way. One of the daughters is getting married. Going to be a big affair. Rudy, up at the store, says he had to order in a lot of extra things."

Peg said, "Hey kids, let's go out in the boat!"

"Let's go across the lake!"

"Too far to row," said Dickie. "Let's get the motor."

"Got any gas?" asked Retta.

"Plenty."

Dickie was good with boats and motors. He could always

start a motor by the third try. He had to get it 'warmed up,' he said. Bree thought the real secret was pulling the starter cord out fast enough.

The cousins were soon far out on the lake. Stars came out. They could see lanterns on the porch of the old stone house.

"Let's go over there on the beach," said Peg. "There's a little park." It was a clearing cut from the pine woods, down the beach from the old house. Dickie cut the motor, and the moment the boat scraped lake bottom, they all jumped into the water and pulled the boat onto the shore.

"Hey, this is swell!" They fell back onto the sand. Bree looked across the lake. "You can see our fire over there. Bet the old folks are sitting right where we left them."

"Ya, but what should we do?"

"Let's play hide-and-seek."

"It'll be too dark."

"No," said Bree, "look there." The top of a pine tree was spearing the rim of a nearly full moon.

"This rock is base," said Retta, "and you're *It*, Dickie!"

"Naw, I ain't!"

Bree knew that Dickie wouldn't dare ask *her* to be It.

"Okay, I'll be It, then," said Peg, who really didn't care anyway, and never came along with them, if she had anything else to do. But Bree knew Peg was curious about the old house and the people who were going to have a wedding.

Peg started counting. Bree moved away on what she thought was a cleared pathway. Her feet weren't as tough as her cousins', but it was a point of honor not to be bothered too much if she stepped on sticks or prickers. It was easy to step on broken glass in parks and, she thought with a shiver, there might be bears in the woods around here. She didn't hear Peg counting anymore. No one else seemed to have come her way. The night was silent except for frogs and crickets and the mosquitoes that kept buzzing like bowing violins in an orchestra. They were bearable only if you didn't run into a swarm headlong. A bombardment of mosquitoes had sent her and her cousins into the lake more than once to escape.

Bree heard shuffling, and a few tree limbs snap. A bear – she thought it could be – and felt her hair stand on end. Then she heard a low murmur that wasn't a bear and a muffled laugh that wasn't Peg. Two figures emerged from the trees and stood not far away in a clearing. Moonlight seemed to fall just on the two of them, and the girl turned her face to the guy. They kissed and then put their arms around each other and kissed some more. Maybe they were the ones getting married tomorrow. Bree dare not let them know she was watching.

Laughing, the girl turned away, but the guy grabbed her, and pressed her to him, crushing her to his chest, cradling her there. The couple stood quite still, his hands on her breasts, the girl not moving away or saying anything, just laughing in a moaning sort of way and then she turned and kissed him again.

Bree felt something strange happen inside herself.

Then Peg called, "Olly, olly, ox-in-free!"

The figures struggled from their embrace and fled out of sight into the woods. Bree had lots to sort out in her mind. She seemed always to discover new angles to any ideas she ever had.

As she found her way back to the rock base, Bree asked,

"Who is It, Peg?"

"We're not gonna play anymore," said Retta. "We better get back."

"What happened?" asked Peg.

"I think I mighta heard bears in the wood!" said Dickie.

"Sure are some around!" said Retta.

"Let's go!" said Dickie.

"I kinda tried to peek into the house," said Peg, "but I couldn't see anything."

Bree remained silent.

The cousins pulled the boat into the water. "Come on, Dickie, rev 'er up!"

Dickie pulled the starter, but the motor wouldn't go.

"Sure we got gas?" asked Retta.

It took five tries before Dickie got the motor started. They headed for the cabin on the other side of the lake, the motor throbbing, the water rocking in soft waves.

The adults were waiting for them by the last embers of the fire. Dickie cut the motor. As soon as the boat touched shore, Bree's mother said, "For heaven's sake, you didn't take any life jackets?" Then she turned to the others: "Did anyone remember a flashlight? It's going to be a good walk in the dark!"

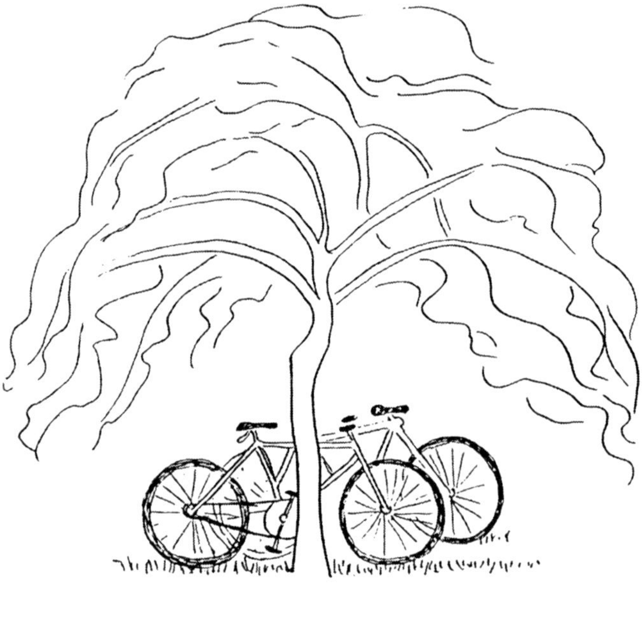

# Weeping Willow

Bree and Betty fixed the bologna sandwiches with lots of mustard, slopping it on, then smoothing off all but a decent amount. They mixed hot sauce into the leftover mustard. "Do you think that's about right?" asked Betty, raising her eyebrow, shaking drips of the hot Tabasco they had secretly purchased, because neither of their mothers used it in the kitchen. "Tasty enough?"

They laughed and spread the mix on half of the sandwiches. "Can you tell from the wrap which sandwiches are ours?" asked Bree.

"We'll put their sandwiches on top!"

"Can't wait to see those guys' faces when they eat..."

"Me either!"

"They will need li-i-quid refreshment!"

"They said they were going to bring apple cider," said Betty.

"What time?"

"Twelve sharp!" Betty was more confident with boys. Bree didn't know why. Maybe it was looks. Bree couldn't compare herself to Betty or Kathy or Ann or—she had a long list. A million times she told herself it didn't matter, yet here she was, once again, making a mess of herself in her mind—on a beautiful autumn Saturday.

~

"Let's spread the blanket by the old willow," said Betty. The willow grew by a drainage ditch that cut through a field in back of Bree's house. The girls lay on the blanket. If Bree stretched her arm, she could pull down sprays of the drooping weeping willow, leaves like the beads of a delicate necklace on a blue sky.

"What time is it?" asked Bree.

"Half past eleven."

"Do you think those boys won't show up?"

"Don't worry, what else better have they got to do? We said we'd bring the sandwiches, didn't we?"

"Yuk!" laughed Bree.

"And I'm hungry!" said Betty, who seemed to Bree to be able to eat all day long and never get fat. Bree was immoderate – she'd got that from Roget's, trying to get a correct definition of herself – excessive. She either ate all the time or starved, dieting. She was either happy all the time or so sad that only a big cry would make her feel good again (but only after the splotchy face and swollen eyelids had withdrawn from the vision in her mirror). She was about to conclude that she really was a *bitch*, that hateful word tossed around in not-so-polite conversation when girls felt adventurous. As they lay back on their elbows on the blanket, Bree asked, "Do you know what 'bitch' really means?"

"What?" asked Betty, mistaking her question for a ready answer.

"I'm asking you!"

"What a bitch is?" Betty shrugged, "I guess it's a female who isn't very nice."

"Also a female dog with pups."

"Or a female in heat?" asked Betty.

Bree guessed that was why she felt so 'bitchy,' she'd just got her period. Felt like a dog! "Sometimes," she said, "I feel lousy!"

"You mean lousy, like lice in your hair?!"

"Yes! Itchy to be doing something special, that's for sure! Do you realize how much time we waste just sitting around?" asked Bree.

"Like right now, you mean? Waiting for the boys to show up?"

"Not that, exactly."

"Well, I'm waiting for Mr. Perfect to show up," said Betty.

"Do you *know* a Mr. Perfect?"

"No," said Betty, "but some of the guys at the high school are really cute."

"I know," said Bree wistfully.

"High school has opened up our prospects."

"Our what?" asked Bree. The girls split into laughter. "Trouble is, all those cute guys don't even look our way. Well, my way, anyway. Maybe yours?"

"Yeh," said Betty, "I'm hopelessly in love!"

"In love?"

"You know that real cute blond in the eleventh grade, the one who wears a varsity sweater with the number three on it?"

Bree nodded. She had looked at him, too, and now waited expectantly for a revelation from Betty.

"Well, the other day he sort of looked at me when he passed in the hall after Math class."

"What do you mean, sort of?"

"You know, he looked at me kind of like, maybe, I wasn't *so* bad to look at."

"What did you do?"

"What *could* I do? I just melted into the floor, that's what!"

They laughed until the tears came. "Stop laughing! I'm serious!" said Betty, rolling in a fit of giggles. Then she sat up. "And you know what?"

"No, what?"

"To add to the melting mess in the hallway, that night I *dreamed* about him! He was walking down the hall, like after Math, but this time he held out his letter sweater to me—and you won't believe this!"

"Yes, I will!" said Bree.

"He pulled his letter sweater right over my head, and I thought in my dream, we were sort of engaged or something!" Giggles again and then Betty continued, "And I felt, well, you know, so great, 'cause he *liked* me, that I nearly fainted!" They laughed again, Betty saying, "Now wait a minute!"—unable to continue until their giggling stopped. "Then he came down the hall again, and I knew he wanted the sweater back, so I pulled it off – and this is the worst – I didn't have anything on underneath! I was naked!"

Laughter again. "Then what?"

"Then he disappeared!" Giggles still. "Was I ever relieved when I woke up and found out it hadn't really happened! And this is worst of all—when I passed him in the hall the next day, he looked at me again, and I turned absolutely red in the face. I was *so* embarrassed!"

"That's great!" said Bree. "That's really crazy! Nothing like that happens to me!"

"What about Craig?"

"He's just a—bother!"

When the girls had calmed their laughing once again, they made a list of the most eligible boyfriends 'to be' at the high school, none of whom were from their class, or anyone to whom they ever had actually spoken. "If only they would look at us!" said Betty.

The girls sat up suddenly. "Is that them?"

"Looks like it!"

Craig and Bob were riding their bikes through the grass from the far side of the field. "Don't they look like a couple of dopes." The boys wore cutoff jeans, sleeveless sweatshirts, sneakers, and navy surplus caps. "Hi, hi!" they said all around.

"What are you doing?"

"Nothing."

The boys propped their bikes against the willow tree. "We thought you guys wouldn't show up," said Bree.

"Had to buy the drinks."

"Didn't you get apple cider?" asked Betty, eyeing the soda bottles they brought.

"Couldn't find any."

"What did you get instead?"

"Cherry soda."

"Yuk," said Bree under her breath, thinking of the tabasco-mustard sandwiches.

"Cherry's great stuff!" said Craig. "Only it's not too cold. Got the coldest pop they had."

"But we brought a dozen donuts," said Bree. "How can we eat donuts without cider?"

"Easy enough," said the boys. "Try us!"

"Hungry already?"

"Sure," they said.

"Let's spread the stuff out on the blanket."

"Great!" said Betty. Out of a grocery bag, she took a sack of potato chips, a box of donuts, and two sandwiches.

"Here's the pop!" said Craig.

"Cherry, yuk!" said Bree again.

"Who's got the bottle opener?" They looked at each other.

"Oh, well," said Craig, tossing his head. "I can always pull the cap off with my teeth!"

"I can lift it with my thumbnail!" said Bob in pantomime.

"I can run home for an opener," volunteered Bree.

"Forget it," said the boys.

"Famous last words," said Betty.

"We don't *drink*, anyway," said Craig, staggering around.

"Let's forget the prelims," said Bob, "and eat!"

"Where are those sandwiches, witches?" asked Craig.

"Eh, he, he!" said Bree, making the most witchy face she could, pointing her eyes toward her nose and thrusting the sandwiches in the boys' direction. The girls sat back on the blanket, watching the boys unwrap their sandwiches.

"What's this?" said Bob. "Pickle and bologna? Great!"

The boys bit into their sandwiches, smiling, then their faces turned to grimaces.

"Wow!" "Fire!" they yelled. Bob waved his hand in front of his mouth as if to put out a flame. Craig jumped around on one foot and then the other. "Ha, ha, ha, hot!" he yelled.

"Great show!" said Bree. "That's what you get for not bringing the bottle opener!"

"Look, you guys," said Betty, raising her sandwich to her mouth, biting in, chewing slowly. "Perfectly delicious!"

"Yummm," said Bree, chewing hers. "Never had better, and the bread is so fresh!"

"Your sandwiches are okay?" asked Bob, waving his tongue between words.

"Delicious!"

"Not hot?"

"Not at all," said Betty, "same as yours." She thumbed open her sandwich for a cursory look from the boys. "I can't understand what's got into you guys!" Then, relenting a bit, she said, "Here, try some donuts!"

The boys took the donuts cautiously and looked them over carefully, eyeing Bree and Betty. Bob sniffed his; Craig twirled a donut around his finger.

"Are you sure you didn't *do* anything to these donuts?"

The girls shook their heads seriously and winked at each other. Bob said, "Well, I think I'll have to eat another donut just to be sure!"

The boys ate all the donuts before Bree and Betty had finished their sandwiches. They remarked more than once, "Boy, that's good!" "Yummm!" "Delish!"

Fighting back their desire for the unopened cherry pop,

they agreed it was time to do something, but what?

“Should I go back to the house for a bottle opener?” asked Bree.

“Let’s do foot-to-foot.” Bree knew Bob would want to do that. The game was played in a circle foot-to-foot, hip-to-hip, arm-to-arm, little finger twist to little finger. It was a game that usually got started when there was a fair number of boys to girls and ended when no one could move anymore or everyone had tumbled to the ground out of balance.

“I’m too full,” said Bree.

“I’m stuffed on those donuts and potato chips,” said Craig.

“Come on,” said Betty. “Let’s play!”

“Let’s play!” said Craig, grabbing Bree by the arm, trying to pull her up from the blanket.

“Stop it, Craig! I really don’t want to! Let’s get some ice at my place.”

The four of them ran through the field, jumping the drainage ditch two-by-two, Craig holding Bree’s hand, pulling her along.

Her mother was in the kitchen. They might have stayed longer and given the boys something better to eat, but Bree didn’t want to explain anything to Mother. She was already asking, “Well, did you have a nice picnic? I know the girls were here in the kitchen a long time fixing sandwiches!”

Craig and Bob looked at each other and said nothing.

“We need a bottle opener and some ice.”

“And paper cups!”

They were soon running across the field again, away from the parental eye in the kitchen. “Hey, watch the ditch!”

“I ought to go out for the sprint,” said Betty, who was running as fast as the boys. Craig turned back to Bree, caught her arm, and swung her with so much momentum across the drainage ditch that she tumbled into a ball at his knees. She’d got a jolt, but stood up laughing. What else could she do? “Hey, watch it!” she said. “I’m not falling for you!”

“Come on,” said Craig, trying to take her arm again. Bree gave him her hand instead. That was ‘safe’ territory. Maybe she should call off the clutching? It wasn’t that she didn’t like Craig. She could talk to him, even if he was a boy. It was just—she didn’t want to have to put up with struggles. But what was happening? Craig had caught her hard, was crushing her chest to his, and was kissing her on the lips! She pushed away, feeling a kind of shock and the moisture of his lips on hers. Craig’s startled eyes looked at her. “Okay?”

“Yeh, sure—okay,” said Bree, looking around for Betty and Bob. “Where are they?”

“Around here someplace,” he said, looking off toward the willow tree. “You see, we made a bet...”

“A bet! No kidding? A bet that both of you...?” Bree laughed. “So it’s really kind of a joke!”

“Sure!” said Craig.

Later, as Bree was describing the ‘puppy dog look’ on Craig’s face, Betty said, “You know what the trouble is?”

“What?” asked Bree.

“Growing pains! They’re sure to get over it—someday!”

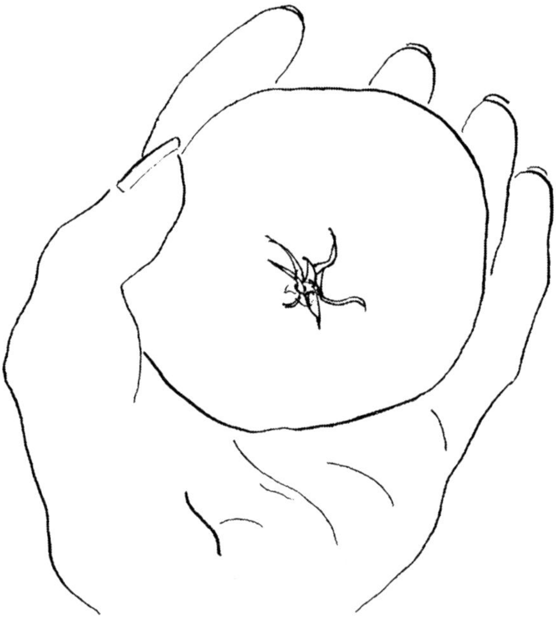

# The Tomato

Bree was part of the talent assembly. She had dressed carefully this morning so that how she looked wouldn't bother her, sitting in the front row of chairs on stage. She wasn't too nervous about singing. She heard on the radio that even Lily Pons was nervous before opera performances. "Being a little nervous is good, makes you sing better," said her music teacher.

It wasn't the singing, really, it was just being there on stage waiting, *thinking* about being there that was the worst. When she sang, she usually forgot herself in a song, anyway. Besides, she'd sung alone before on this stage and it hadn't been a disaster. Some kids even said they *liked* her song. "A bowl of roses," she had sung, "languishing, glorying, glowing their life away..." She sang slowly, deliberately, holding out the phrases. It was almost as if she were explaining herself. But the song was dull to a bunch of, oh, she couldn't think of it, but yes, the song was dull to a bunch of *dullards*. That was a great new word for her vocabulary.

But where was she in this program? She would have to pay attention, keep her mind from wandering. She read down the list. She must be next in order, as John, sitting next to her, was strapping his accordion to his shoulders, unfastening the clasp of what he ceremoniously called 'my piano accordion.' John pushed up his silver-rimmed glasses and walked to center stage. The spotlight was on him.

The magic moment. John pulled apart what the kids called his 'squeezebox' and filled its lungs with air. He played his accordion in a popular polka band, but today he had chosen a 'serious' piece to play. Bree thought he was quite good. But at the end, John received slight applause. She wondered if that bothered him or not, because he never changed expression.

The school principal broke into the program with a few announcements. Bree looked over the stage lights. Beyond the first row, it was hard to distinguish anyone. Even in the front row, a yellow haze seemed to change people into strangers, statues staring ahead. But there was plenty of movement in that row. Unless you were early in the program, restlessness set into the kids.

There was Craig in the front row. Why was he up there? He looked like he was looking at her and then he raised his arm, something in his hand. Yes, it was – she felt her blood rise in fury – it was a tomato, and he was waving it in front of her. She knew why. On their last date he had said, "But Bree, why are you such a cold tomato?"

How could she have explained that she didn't want to kiss him? Diplomatically? Was he waving that tomato now to tease her? He must have brought it in his lunch on purpose. Was it possible he really didn't like her anymore? Was he going to throw that tomato at her if her singing wasn't good?

John's elbow punched her arm. Bree turned and noticed that the principal was looking at her. She hadn't heard a thing and now it was her turn!

"Come," she whispered to Donna, her accompanist. "Let's face the music!"

They strode out on the stage—maybe, thought Bree, to a firing squad. She mustn't be grim, with Craig sitting there, or laugh either. She saw from the corner of her eye a wave of that tomato. She would ignore it. She turned to Donna, who sat at the piano, pages spread and arranged for easy turning. Bree nodded for Donna to begin.

The introduction—Bree felt her lungs fill, feeling as if she might soar, but held the breath back of the first notes, firm, yet soft in attack.

"The game of just pretending is"—her voice flowed easily from note to note. She wondered fleetingly why she had chosen *this* song, and then forgot herself as she sang into the words—"the sweetest game I know-o. ...Our dreams are more romantic, than the world we see."

At those words, she came up from the song just long enough to glare at Craig.

"And if the things we dream about don't happen to be so-o" ...and here Donna played nicely on the keys, slowing ever so slightly... "That's just an unimportant tech-ni-cal-i-ty." (Softly, intensely, thought Bree.)

Now she could let go and sing out in a romantic slush of words. "We could make believe I love you..."

Her breath flowed in and out without effort. She felt wonderful. She wouldn't make believe. She would be – well – who she really was.

Ina Yount Whitlock
was born and raised in Lincoln, Nebraska.
She has lived and traveled around the world, and for the last quarter century has resided on Vashon Island in the state of Washington, where she continues to write stories and poems, and create art.

Photo by Christina Winge

CPSIA information can be obtained at www.ICGtesting.com
Printed in the USA
BVOW031445041012

302111BV00007B/4/P

9 780985 992903